"Coach Carroll has taught me that to be a true competitor, a true warrior, a person must master one's own doubts, passions, and fears to obtain self-knowledge—self-knowledge being one of the greatest virtues an athlete can attain."

—Troy Polamalu, safety, Pittsburgh Steelers

"Coach Carroll will forever be remembered as one of the best coaches in the history of college football. Even though we may find ourselves on opposite sides of the field now that he's back in the NFL, I can't thank Pete enough for everything he taught me during my last two years at USC and helping me become the player I am today."

—Carson Palmer, quarterback, Cincinnati Bengals

"Pete Carroll taught me what it takes to compete at a high level. He believed in me, and in those three years I started for him at USC, we accomplished things that no other team will ever accomplish. Because of Coach Carroll, his Win Forever philosophy, and how he prepared us, we never once felt the pressure of being on top."

—Matt Leinart, quarterback, Arizona Cardinals

"Coach Carroll is the fiercest competitor I know. Not only as a coach, but also as a mentor and, more important, a friend. That mentality allowed me to enter the NFL with the tools necessary for the highest level of competition. Those traits transcended the field and will offer a competitive edge for anyone who reads his book."

—Mark Sanchez, quarterback, New York Jets

"Sitting in the film room one day at Arkansas, coach Lou Holtz asked me what I thought of our twenty-five-year-old graduate assistant, who happened to be sitting in the back of the room taking notes. My response was short and simple, 'Coach, get to know this young man because he won't be here very long—he's born to be a head coach.' The Seattle Seahawks are fortunate to get Pete Carroll, not just the excellent coach that you will read about in *Win Forever*, but the great person."

—Monte Kiffin, legendary defensive coordinator

"The thing that impresses me the most about Coach Carroll is that he practices what he preaches, as he is both the student and the teacher. He lives his life, both on and off the field, with passion, enthusiasm, integrity, a can-do attitude, a tireless work ethic, and a heart of gold. Coach Carroll lives his Win Forever philosophy, and the results of choosing such a life are beautiful, inspiring, and wonderfully successful."

—Kerri Walsh, two-time Olympic Gold medalist and the world's top-ranked women's volleyball player

"The teachings of Coach Carroll are universal and stretch beyond athletics into all aspects of life. *Win Forever* is a must read for anyone looking to maximize his or her potential and live a richer and more fulfilled life."　　—Dean Karnazes, ultramarathoner and *New York Times* bestselling author of *50/50*

"Pete's infectious passion for the game of football, his competitive edge, and his zest for life are a reminder to us all that it's the journey and not the destination that counts. I have been inspired by his enthusiasm, impressed by his professionalism, and challenged to become an even better coach and person myself thanks to his example."

—Jürgen Klinsmann, international soccer icon and former Germany World Cup and Bayern Munich manager/coach

"Pete Carroll's fiery effervescence burns through this book with marvelous clarity and wisdom. *Win Forever* will inspire men and women young and old for a long, long time to come. Its integration of sport and high, hard-won philosophy opens new ways for us into our own undiscovered country."

—Michael Murphy, founder of the Esalen Institute, author of *Golf in the Kingdom* and *The Future of the Body*

"*Win Forever* is not about sports, it is about life. Pete has found a way to create a vision that instills character and integrity through the competition that we call life. It is about how we choose to see the world, our life, and the problems within both, and find a way to have faith and confidence that we have it within ourselves to solve these problems."

—Tim Leiweke, president and CEO, AEG

WIN FOREVER

WIN FOREVER

LIVE, WORK, AND PLAY
LIKE A CHAMPION

PETE CARROLL

WITH YOGI ROTH

AND KRISTOFFER A. GARIN

PORTFOLIO

PORTFOLIO
Published by the Penguin Group
Penguin Group (USA) Inc., 375 Hudson Street,
New York, New York 10014, U.S.A.
Penguin Group (Canada), 90 Eglinton Avenue East, Suite 700,
Toronto, Ontario, Canada M4P 2Y3 (a division of Pearson Penguin Canada Inc.)
Penguin Books Ltd, 80 Strand, London WC2R 0RL, England
Penguin Ireland, 25 St. Stephen's Green, Dublin 2, Ireland
(a division of Penguin Books Ltd)
Penguin Books Australia Ltd, 250 Camberwell Road, Camberwell,
Victoria 3124, Australia (a division of Pearson Australia Group Pty Ltd)
Penguin Books India Pvt Ltd, 11 Community Centre, Panchsheel Park,
New Delhi—110 017, India
Penguin Group (NZ), 67 Apollo Drive, Rosedale, North Shore 0632,
New Zealand (a division of Pearson New Zealand Ltd)
Penguin Books (South Africa) (Pty) Ltd, 24 Sturdee Avenue,
Rosebank, Johannesburg 2196, South Africa

Penguin Books Ltd, Registered Offices:
80 Strand, London WC2R 0RL, England

First published in 2010 by Portfolio,
a member of Penguin Group (USA) Inc.

1   3   5   7   9   10   8   6   4   2

Copyright © Win Forever, LLC, 2010
All rights reserved

Library of Congress Cataloging-in-Publication Data

Carroll, Pete, 1951–
Win forever : live, work, and play like a champion / Pete Carroll with
Yogi Roth and Kristoffer A. Garin.
p.   cm.
Includes index.
ISBN 978-1-59184-323-8
1. Success.   2. Excellence.   3. Sports.   I. Roth, Yogi.   II. Title.
GV965.C414 2010
796—dc22   2010011848

Printed in the United States of America
Set in Minion Pro
Designed by Victoria Hartman

To Glena, Brennan, Jaime, and Nate,
who have allowed me to chase
the dream all these years

Contents

Part Three

WIN FOREVER AT USC

10. Getting the Job at USC 95
11. Laying Ground Rules 102
12. Coach Your Coaches 116
13. Coaches Are Teachers 127
14. Our Approach to Practice 138
15. Fourth and Nine 152
16. Our Recruiting Promise 161
17. Making It Fun 167
18. Playing in the Absence of Fear 177
19. Setting a Vision and Seeing It 183
20. Winning Forever On and Off the Field 189

Part Four

WIN FOREVER BEYOND THE FIELD

21. Not Just Football 199
22. You Can Win Forever 207
Conclusion 215

Acknowledgments 221
Index 225

WIN FOREVER

INTRODUCTION

I slammed the book shut, stunned.

It had been six months since I'd been fired as the head coach of the New England Patriots and in the summer of 2000 I was trying to figure out what to do next with my life. I was reading a book by the legendary basketball coach John Wooden.

It took him sixteen years to figure it out, I told myself, *but once he did, he absolutely knew it. After that, he rarely lost, and he went on to win ten of the next twelve national championships. It seemed he won forever.*

Looking back, I had been feeling all but down and out. Suddenly everything had changed.

I reached for a pad of paper and started writing. What Coach Wooden had done that so impressed me was to pull together his own vision, philosophy, and belief system into a detailed plan for winning. Once he had it, he went on, year after year, to build teams that were almost unstoppable. I needed to come up with a plan of my own. I needed to develop my own winning philosophy and design a plan for implementing it. I started that afternoon.

For the next few hours, days, and weeks I wrote down phrases, bullet points, and definitions about who I was, where I had been, where I wanted to go, and what I wanted the next program I ran to look like. In no particular order, I wrote what came to mind. It was completely unorganized, but I knew just getting it all down on paper was a critical first step.

I embarked on a process of discovering who I was, not only as a football coach but, more important, as a person. At one point I leaned back in my chair, football in hand, and smiled. I couldn't believe that I had been coaching for the past twenty-six years and had never stated my philosophy, let alone written it down.

The process was long and difficult, but the more I wrote, the more powerful the experience became. Finally, I made a breakthrough. I realized that at the core of my being, I was a competitor. I had been competing my entire life at everything. With this understanding, I set about structuring a football program strictly based upon my core belief. Competition would become the central theme of the program, and our day-to-day thinking would be driven by this single thought: to do things better than they had ever been done before. I was making real progress solidifying my philosophy and was truly excited about how things were coming together.

My entire life and coaching career were about to change. After coaching sixteen years in the National Football League, I had decided to return to the collegiate level and pursue a head-coaching position. When the University of Southern California called and asked me to interview for their opening, I realized that this was a chance to unveil my philosophy. The job was offered and I accepted. A once proud and traditionally powerful football program had fallen on hard times, and now it was my turn to take over.

Throughout the hiring process I sensed a newfound confidence and belief in myself. I had never felt so prepared and well equipped to deal with the challenges of taking over a program. Coach Wooden's example inspired me to create a vision and a philosophy that would become the foundation of the USC football program.

After two seasons we had become Pacific 10 Conference Champions, won the Orange Bowl following the 2002 season, and watched quarterback Carson Palmer receive the coveted Heisman Trophy in New York City. We were on our way to becoming one of the most dominant football programs in the country. During my nine years at USC we went on to win seven straight Pac-10 titles, appear in seven straight Bowl Championship Series games, win two national championships, have three Heisman Trophy winners, and set an all-time record for being ranked as the number one team in the Associated Press poll for thirty-three straight weeks.

Our success at USC began with the philosophy I refer to now as *Win Forever*. It is an approach that allowed us to sustain high-level championship performance over a record-breaking period. What might appear to be a philosophy targeted primarily on wins and losses was in fact a vehicle for maximizing team and individual performance. We were in the midst of a great run, with hopefully no end in sight.

After the 2009 season, I was in the midst of solidifying our upcoming recruiting class, when I received a call to interview for the head coaching position from Tod Leiweke, the CEO of the Seattle Seahawks. Initially, the interview was similar to meetings that I had had in the past with various NFL teams, but I soon realized that this opportunity might be different. It did not sound like a typical sales pitch. His words and his tone had a depth to them, a sincerity and a sense of legitimacy. Tod and owner Paul Allen assured me that I would have all the control and support I would need from the organization, similar to the situation I already had at USC.

It was difficult to think about leaving USC, but the opportunity to take the Win Forever philosophy to the NFL was compelling. In Seattle I would have the chance to compete at the highest level in football and I was fired up about the prospects of that happening. It was becoming clear that this opportunity in the NFL could be a perfect fit, a situation that, up until now, I didn't think existed for me. I spoke to my family and close friends and considered the impact this would have on everyone around me. This was one of the most difficult decisions I ever had to make, and it helped knowing my wife, Glena, and our family supported me either way.

The Seahawks called back and offered the job. They told me they wanted me to bring the philosophy and the approach that had been so instrumental at USC. After careful thought and consideration, I called Tod Leiweke and said I was ready to go. It is amazing how your life can change so suddenly.

Taking the step to return to the NFL may have seemed daunting to some people and certainly has been challenged by others, possibly due to the fact that during a lengthy career in the league, I had been fired twice from head coaching positions. Since then questions had been raised repeatedly about whether my style and approach fit more appropriately in college than in the pros. However, upon returning to the high-risk world of the NFL, I could not be more excited or more confident about coming back.

The last time I was hired as a head coach in the league was 1997. That was a different time and place and so much has happened since then. This time around, I see things differently. The wealth of experience and all that has taken place since that time has changed me. The process of self-discovery that was necessary to formulate my vision, and the power of having a philosophy has given me a confidence I didn't have before. One of the keys to success lies in knowing and believing in yourself. When you are confident and you trust in who you are, you can perform to the best of your ability, and that is exactly what I plan to do. Whether you are coaching the USC Trojans or the Seattle Seahawks, working at your job or running a household, all you should ever strive for is to be the best you can be . . . and that is the essence of what it means to Win Forever.

PART ONE

BEFORE THE PHILOSOPHY

1

BEGINNING TO COMPETE

As a kid growing up in Marin County, California, I was more or less like all the other kids interested in sports: I just wanted to play. I never dreamed of becoming a coach.

It did not matter what season it was, or what sport—it could even be a game that we made up on the spot—the competition was always on. In our close-knit neighborhood, we played in the shadow of Mount Tamalpais and on nearby school playgrounds. As far back as I can remember, I was always battling with my friends to be the best at all the things I enjoyed. I took great pride in excelling in all sports as I moved through Kentfield-Greenbrae Little League, Pop Warner football, and whatever else I could find to test my abilities. I knew that when I finally got to high school I was going to do well. There was no doubt in my mind.

Unfortunately, my body at the time had other ideas. In spite of my youthful confidence, my physical development was slow and was not cooperating with my ambitions. While other kids experienced growth spurts and puberty, I still had a ways to go. I entered Redwood High School as a five-foot-four-inch, 110-pound freshman needing a doctor's note in order to be cleared to play football. I had passion and a fiercely competitive spirit, but that could take me only so far. Guys I would never have considered my competition were suddenly the ones to beat.

This period was one of my first real encounters with disappointment. I hated being told that no matter what I did I would not be good enough to compete to be the best at something I loved. But there was no denying the limitations I was facing as an athlete. As I moved from the ranks of Little League and Pop Warner to the more competitive arena of high school sports, my lack of size made it difficult to excel like I wanted. It seemed that the only thing about me that was growing at the time was the chip on my shoulder.

My frustrations were probably shared by the members of my family, but they were nonetheless loving and supportive. The lessons I learned from them and the other people who remained closest to me at the time continue to play a large role in my personal and professional development today.

My mom and dad were always there for me. They went to every game that I ever played, and they were the best kind of Little League parents. They expected me to play hard and to do my best, but they never made me feel pressured or afraid of failing. Their support was something I always felt. I knew that I could count on them.

My mother was a great influence on my values and outlook. She was a real giver, and throughout my childhood our house was always open to my friends. It was a fun stop for everyone, and it became a way station for a lot of kids as we were growing up. Some of my friends would stop by to talk with her even when I was not there. My friends and I felt close to both of my parents, and my mother especially was always available as a sounding board for whatever ideas we had. She instilled in me a great curiosity about how the world works, along with an overall sense of optimism and possibility. She used to say: "Something good is just about to happen." I still believe that today.

My dad was extraordinarily competitive and showed that often as a boisterous fan. But when it came to me, I only had great support from him. He was smart and tenacious, and whether he was playing cards, golf, or board games, it didn't matter—he was going to win. I did not realize it at the time, but looking back it's obvious that's who he was and what he was all about. I always hate to reduce people to a single dimension, but when you get right down to it, my dad was first and foremost an extraordinary competitor, and my mom was about as open and giving as someone could be.

In classic little-brother fashion I worshipped my big brother, Jim, who was five years older and would follow him around like a puppy dog whenever he let me. He was a three-sport star growing up and in high school. His friends would mentor me, and I would imitate them in everything: how they shot a basketball, threw a football, or stood in the batter's box. Jim would go on to teach me the finest points of gamesmanship and competitive tactics that most little kids in Marin were not exposed to. By the time I entered Little League I probably had an edge. I knew how to hook slide, pop-up slide, and hit the dirt and go in headfirst. My pitching arsenal was also growing as I was taught how to throw a curveball, slider, change-up, and knuckleball, to name a few. When most kids in town were watching *The Mickey Mouse Club* on television, I was watching Jim and his friends compete at whatever sport was in season—it didn't matter. I wanted to be like Jim, but I also vividly recall wanting to beat him at something, just one time. I guess I felt if I could beat my older brother, my hero, just once, I would know I could beat anybody. It seems a little over the top how hard I would try to beat them; my brother and his friends would crack up over it, and looking back, I can't blame them.

The support that I got early in life did not come just from my family. My early coaches were also great sources of guidance and motivation. We may have been playing "little league," but I can tell you that my Pop Warner coaches were seriously tough and demanding. Even though we were very young, they made us understand that we had to put in our best effort if we wanted to be part of the sport. All of them helped to teach me that when you are trying to do something really well, the stakes are always high: You're either competing to be the best you can be or you're not.

At the end of my freshman year, my high school coach, Bob Troppmann, invited me to work at his summer Pop Warner football camp as an instructor, assistant coach, and all-around helping hand. It was a huge moment in my development as a young competitor. Working and coaching the kids for a week would earn me the right to attend Coach's two-week high school summer camp, the Diamond B, for free. I would have happily done more than that for the opportunity.

The opportunity meant a lot to me, as the Diamond B was known in our world as a boot camp for aspiring football players. And it was the real thing: The rustic setting and bare-bones facility located in the hills outside Boonville, California, was where Coach T, a proud marine, gave me my start. Coach T may not have been able to make me taller, but he definitely toughened me up. The days started with early-morning wake-up calls to the tune of the "Marines' Hymn" and five-mile runs and included grueling two-a-day practices that would set the tone for what football was all about for me. I loved every minute of it. Looking back, I see that working at Coach T's Pop Warner camp and participating in the Diamond B camp gave me an early start in coaching; I just didn't realize it at the time.

Like any kid, I had heroes, and most of mine were athletes. Growing up outside San Francisco in the late 1960s was exciting, and I was interested in a lot of what was going on around us. But especially in high school, my life revolved around sports. I played baseball, basketball, and football throughout my high school years. I worshipped Gale Sayers of the Chicago Bears as one of the greatest open-field runners of all time and the NBA legend Rick Barry for his unwavering confidence and his understanding of who he was as an athlete. My favorite idol was San Francisco Giants Hall of Fame baseball player Willie Mays. Even today I feel blessed to have had the chance to cheer for Willie, one of the greatest performers of all time.

I could not have imagined back then how many of those heroes I would actually have the chance to meet and even work with someday. I had a poster hanging on my bedroom wall of Sayers and Mike Garrett from their days as star players in the NFL. If you had told me then how closely Mike and I would become connected in the years to follow, I would have called you crazy. I never would have thought that Mike would be my boss one day—as the USC athletic director, he was the one who hired me as the coach of the Trojans, and we worked together closely for nine seasons. At the time, I just wanted to play the same game they did.

During my high school years, I never lived up to my desires and expectations as an athlete even though I competed more or less non-stop. I played baseball, basketball, and football all four years, but I was never really satisfied with my play. My coaches saw my frustration. I clearly had a passion and competitive spirit that separated me from others. I was arriving early to practice, staying late, and essentially always looking to find a competitive edge. I just couldn't seem to find one. Nevertheless, by my senior year, I was taking the field for Coach Troppmann on a steady basis. I remember one occasion that year when he put me in at quarterback late in the game against

Santa Rosa High School, essentially to mop things up. In those days we called our own plays, and all the guys in the huddle were begging me to throw the ball to them. Coach T had told me specifically not to throw the ball and just call running plays. Instead I called a pass to one of my receivers and their defensive back intercepted it. On the interception return, I tried to tackle him on the sideline, but he got around me and ran in for a touchdown. I'll always remember the sight of Coach standing over me as I opened my eyes, lying there in the mud. "Carroll," he said, "you're on my black list." Eventually he let me off the hook and forgave me. To this day, I still call Coach T from the sidelines before every game we play. I don't think we've missed one of those conversations in years.

What I didn't know was that those disappointing years in high school sports would prove to be invaluable when I entered the coaching circuit later in life. When I left Redwood High as an eager seventeen-year-old graduate, a career in coaching was the furthest thing from my mind. I wanted to be a player, and after a long wait, my body was finally starting to catch up.

With aspirations of still making a significant mark as an athlete, I entered junior college at the College of Marin to improve my game as a football player—along with my grades, which were less than stellar coming out of Redwood. At Marin, at long last, I started to become the player that I always had hoped to be and I started to get recognized. After two years at Marin, I was awarded a scholarship to play safety for the University of the Pacific in Stockton, California. At the time, UOP had a reputable Division I football program under Coach Homer Smith and, in my final year, Coach Chester Caddas. It was a dream come true for me. In a two-year career at UOP, I received recognition as an All-Coast and All-Conference player—the first time since before high school that I had received recognition for my play. It was a chance to reclaim my personal identity as a real athlete and performer, and I will forever be grateful to Pacific for my days playing there. The opportunities I had there literally changed the direction of my life forever.

My career as a UOP Tiger may not have propelled me into the NFL to play alongside personal heroes like the guys on my wall, but it did open important doors for me. From Pacific, I was invited to training camp with the Honolulu Hawaiians of the World Football League. I recognized from the beginning that it was a "world" away from the real thing, but here was a chance to play professional football. Instead of having training camp in the team's home city or some other exotic place, we were relegated to hot and smoggy Riverside, California, but I didn't care. Although it was going to be difficult to break in, even to this league, I was determined to make the most of it. I resolved to put everything I had into that fall camp.

Unfortunately, I would be disappointed. Due to an NFL players' strike just two weeks into my tryout with the Hawaiians, WFL rosters across the country were suddenly jammed with NFL players looking for work. These guys were literally in a different league, and competing with them was going to be close to impossible. Combine that unlucky timing with a nasty shoulder injury in practice, and it was all but inevitable that my professional career would be brief.

The beginning of the end of my professional career actually came on our very first day of practice. The coaches had me playing at free safety, and in spite of the fact that we were not playing in full pads, I was ready to prove that I could tackle and hit wide receivers harder than anybody there. As that first practice continued, I was gaining confidence and having a blast. During our final team period of the day, the offense completed a pass down the sideline and I moved aggressively to cut off the receiver. Just before the goal line, I was about to hammer the receiver, but he stumbled and I dove over him instead, landing hard. It seemed as if it were all in slow motion, and I can still hear my shoulder crunching as I hit the turf.

The trainer diagnosed me with a mild shoulder sprain, said I was okay, and ordered a few days' rest. As soon as he agreed, I was back on the field competing for a roster spot. I was far from being healed, and in hindsight I can see that maybe it was a mistake, but at the time I wasn't going to let anyone or anything get between me and my dream.

Unfortunately, I was already going against better players than the ones I had played against at Pacific. With my shoulder banged up, I lost the punch I needed to strike receivers and tight ends the way I knew how. They just weren't going down as easily as they had back in college. Two weeks into camp, in what ended up being my final practice with the Hawaiians, a golden opportunity presented itself. The tight end ran a beautiful corner route, and just as he was about to make the catch, I jumped to knock it down. I fell a few inches short and he ended up scoring a touchdown. As he was making the catch, something inside of me said, *Pete, this may be your last play as a professional.* I wish that voice had been wrong.

Early the next morning, the administrative assistant for the Hawaiians knocked on my door and said, "Coach needs to see you. . . . And bring your playbook." I walked toward the head coach's office, knowing my fate, and I sat down expecting to meet him. Rather, one of the assistants was there to greet me. "Pete, we know you're a really good player, but with your speed we think you're not going to be fast enough, so we're going to release you."

I was crushed by the news and to this day it still bothers me. I had worked so hard to beat the odds, and then, just as I was making my way toward competing at an elite level, my career was over. It all seemed to happen so fast and I was devastated. I have never completely accepted that it didn't work out for me as a player, and to this day I still wish I could suit up. I really do think that if there was a professional league for "old guys," I would go for it in a second. Maybe that chip I had on my shoulder as a kid has never gone away.

After being released, I went back home with absolutely no plan. I never dreamed I would get cut, and I think I was probably a bit in shock about it. As I thought about what would be my next move, a man who had seen me compete for two straight years came calling, and that call changed my life forever. It came from Chester Caddas, one of my head coaches and early mentors at Pacific. When he heard that I had been cut from the Hawaiians, he offered me the chance to come back to the UOP program as a graduate assistant coach to further my education and pursue a master's degree. He gave me a shot at a coaching career and I took it before he had the chance to change his mind. My playing days had ended, and instead of my finding a career, my career had begun to find me. The education and development behind my coaching officially began that day and in the words of my mother, something good was just about to happen.

2

LEARNING TO COACH

My three years studying and working for Chester Caddas at the University of the Pacific brought experiences and lessons that I never could have anticipated. There were challenges and setbacks, but they helped me understand new ways to compete. I was still bothered about not being able to take the field as a player in the way I'd imagined and expected, but at Pacific, both as a young coach and as a graduate student, I was learning faster than ever before.

It didn't take long before I was competing as intensely and passionately in my new role as I ever had on the field as a player. Academically, I was focused on two objectives: to earn a secondary teaching credential that would qualify me to teach and coach on the high school level, and to take classes in a master's program in physical education. My studies led me to my first encounter with sports psychology and performance. The lessons I learned there have become invaluable to me as a coach. The opportunity to be a graduate student while coaching Division I football was one of the greatest experiences I could have had at the time.

When I wasn't consumed by my coaching responsibilities, I found myself immersed in the teachings of various psychologists and authorities on sports performance. Many of these have influenced my personal philosophy and approach ever since. I will always be grateful to Professor Glen Albaugh, who taught sports psychology and served as one of my academic advisers. Dr. Albaugh challenged our class with ideas that transformed forever the way I looked at performance, competition, and coaching.

Abraham Maslow was the first of the big thinkers introduced to us by Dr. Albaugh. Maslow conceptualized a school of thought that emerged in the 1950s as a new, more positive way of thinking about the human personality, its potential, and its needs. He worked until shortly before his death in 1970 and produced a huge body of writing, including some of the early foundations of what would grow into the self-help movement. His classic book *Toward a Psychology of Being* became a foundation for me. I am not sure I would be the coach, or the person, I am today if I had not been exposed to Maslow's principles.

He illustrated the "hierarchy of needs" and the concept of "self-actualization," which left a lasting impression on me. In a nutshell, Maslow said that humans have categories of needs and that these needs—from basic survival to love and friendship—are arranged not randomly but according to a specific order, like a staircase or a ladder. More important, they can only be truly satisfied in sequence. Unless you are able to meet the needs on a lower step, you cannot successfully address the needs on the next step up.

Maslow's sequence begins with physical needs, such as food, water, sleep, etc., and goes on to include less basic needs like safety, community, and love. Someone dying of starvation, Maslow liked to explain, is unlikely to be thinking about love—while someone who is drowning will probably forget about how hungry he is in a hurry. Like so many great discoveries and insights, a lot of what Maslow said seemed like common sense once he pointed it out.

The top level of Maslow's ladder is what he called the level of self-actualization. This is the level where a person's basic needs have all been met to the degree where he or she is liberated to go out and make an impact on the world.

It is also the point where people, in a host of different ways, begin to strive to be the best people they can possibly be. When we reach this level, we can begin to have access to what Maslow called "peak experiences," or moments of great happiness and high performance. At this point people can begin to actualize moments of full potential.

From a coaching perspective, one aspect of Maslow's findings influenced how I looked at players. Maslow is widely considered to have been the first psychologist to study happy, healthy people—from regular folks to extraordinary minds like Albert Einstein. He wanted to understand how they were able to be happy and successful in their lives. I was intrigued by that thought and would begin to look at my players with that new perspective.

What I learned about Maslow's insights challenged me to start asking: *What if my job as a coach isn't so much to force or coerce performance as it is to create situations where players develop the confidence to set their talents free and pursue their potential to its full extent? What if my job as a coach is really to prove to these kids how good they already are, how good they could possibly become, and that they are truly capable of high-level performance?*

As an athlete and a young coach coming from a conventional football background, this concept did not just challenge my early beliefs about coaching—it changed them forever. Maslow was thinking about individual development when he was writing, but the implications for team sports and leadership in general could be groundbreaking. I had grown up in the world of traditional football, where this kind of thinking would have been laughed right out of the locker room. But for some lucky reason Maslow's teachings sank in and stuck with me as I moved on in my coaching career. Clearly, as a coach, I wouldn't be able to control every aspect of my players' lives, but Maslow started me thinking about the entire notion of leadership and motivation in a new way.

At Pacific during those times, winning wasn't exactly a given. But I kept asking myself, *What if players were able to perform exactly how they envisioned themselves performing?*

Fortunately someone with an answer to that question came to visit our class. His name was Tim Gallwey, author of *The Inner Game of Tennis.* Tim, who later became a personal friend of mine, captured my attention instantly. He spoke to us about performance and how an athlete can elevate his performance by mastering the art of playing with a "quieted mind." Tim's insights would be as important to my outlook in the years ahead as any other single influence.

One night during a spring semester, a few of us were invited to have dinner with Tim in San Francisco. We spent a long night talking about the power of our minds and how that factors into performance. I left dinner counting the days until I could try his approach with our UOP players. This was my early introduction to the principles of the Inner Game.

One of the great things about working and studying in northern California during that time was the accessibility to innovative thinking that made me look at the world in a new way. On the field, we executed hard-nosed old-school football, as represented by the program Coach Caddas built at Pacific. We were about discipline, tradition, and toughness—and it worked some of the time. In the classroom, we were working just as hard but looking at athletic performance through a different lens.

One of my first experiments challenging traditional thinking was not so well received by the head coach. We weren't a very good team and we struggled. On a whim, at one of our nightly position meetings, I decided to ask the defensive backs what they thought they needed to get better. And so I went around the room and asked each player the same question. Listening to their suggestions, I took notes and decided to restructure the next day's practice. It was the first time we had really connected as a group, and it was a powerful meeting that left us looking forward to practicing the next day and the prospect of getting better.

When the meeting was over, I headed back to the coaching offices, proud of our meeting. The first person I ran into was Coach Caddas. Still charged up, I said, "Coach, you won't believe what a great meeting we just had!" I started to tell him about it, and as I got to the part about asking the players what they thought they needed, he cut me off. Just when I was expecting praise, he looked me straight in the eye and said in his southern drawl, "Don't you ever ask the players what they need. Don't you ever tell the players that you'll plan practice the way they want it, not as long as you're here on this staff coaching the game of football."

Of course I was crushed—I thought I had such a great moment, and here was my head coach, the man I played for in college, telling me I had made the biggest mistake ever. Still, the next day I found a way to structure practice to meet the needs of my players, and I think we got better after that.

Coach Caddas is a great guy and an excellent coach. It's just that listening to the ideas of the players was not the kind of thing that was done in old-school football. In many cases it's still not done today. But on a basic level, even then, I understood that whether or not that was the "way it was done," I had made a special connection with the players. I had discovered the power of communicating with and listening to those you hope to help. If I was going to do something special and help players find their potential, I was going to have to build relationships and follow my instincts. No matter the result or reprimand, I wanted to hang on to who I was and what I stood for, and follow my heart.

Another person who had an incredible impact on my way of thinking was Michael Murphy, cofounder of the Esalen Institute. He also was a guest lecturer in Professor Albaugh's sports psychology class. He combined ideas from Western psychology and Eastern philosophy in new and exciting ways that I believe still resonate today.

Michael was one of the first researchers to explore the transformational potential of sport, not only in terms of performance but also in terms of how those experiences can drive you to be the best human being you can be. He spoke to our class about the power of an athlete's mind and how he or she could train it to perform in what he called "the zone." He shared story after story that stretched my perceptions about the levels of performance we could achieve through sport.

For the first time in my life, I was truly inspired to study and learn, as the academic subjects were finally set in the context of athletics and performance, things about which I was truly passionate. All of a sudden, I felt like a sponge trying to soak up as much as possible. But by far, the best part was how much it all seemed to apply directly to my job as a coach. Everything that got me excited in the classroom was taken back to the field, meeting room, and locker room. Armed with a newfound sense of confidence and a deeper understanding of the world around me, I began to apply this new knowledge to the way I coached at Pacific.

One small but telling example of how bringing the lessons from the classroom worked occurred during my second season coaching at UOP. Hoping to inject a little energy into my position group, I decided to throw out the wildly unrealistic goal that we could lead the nation in interceptions that year. If ever there was going to be a test of whether mind over matter actually worked, it seemed like this would be it.

On a purely practical level, there was no reason for anyone in their right mind to think that this bunch of guys could accomplish such a lofty goal under the circumstances. We were an ordinary football program, having finished the previous season 5-6-1. We were young and very average athletically, but at the time it didn't seem to matter. We decided to take our shot and see if we could make it happen. There wasn't any reason to believe we would be successful, but there wasn't any reason not to take a shot at something special anyway.

It wasn't something we blew out of proportion—in fact, many of the guys who played for us that season might not even remember it. But for me that goal was always there in the background, not as a boast but as an affirmation: a true statement about what we thought the future could hold for us if we really, truly did our best. Nobody knew and few really cared, but the UOP Tigers had twenty-five interceptions that season, finishing as one of the nation's leaders in interceptions. Who knows exactly *why* we pulled that off. Looking back, I wonder what would have happened had we not set our sights so high. It was an accomplishment worth being proud of, and it gave me confidence that maybe I was onto something. Maybe Maslow, Gallwey, Murphy, and friends really did know what they were talking about.

That defensive success at UOP may not have translated to a championship season, but it absolutely laid the groundwork for my young coaching career. Based on my studies and experiences, I knew that the first step to doing great things was affirming the belief that great things are possible. This is something I came to understand, but it would not be until years later that I would hear someone articulate this principle in the language in which I think about it today. That person would be Lou Tice, founder of the Pacific Institute, based in Seattle.

Lou has been one of my great friends and mentors over the years. As an educator, thinker, and life coach, he has pioneered ways to help individuals and organizations, from major corporations to the United States military, work together more effectively. Many years after that season at UOP, watching Lou help others to function at higher and higher levels helped me put into words what I'd known instinctively back then: that the simple act of making thoughtful, affirmative statements about who we are and what we want to achieve can be an incredibly powerful tool for getting the best possible performance out of ourselves.

All in all, it was an exciting time for me. Some attempts to incorporate new ideas into my coaching, such as the goal of leading the nation in interceptions, were successful. Others didn't go over so well, at least not with Coach Caddas. I was young, and Coach was probably right to see my thinking as a little too progressive for his program, so I followed and respected his lead. All the same, the ideas that came out of my studies stayed with me, and I looked forward to the day when I could try them out in a new environment.

Around this time Bob Cope, an assistant coach at Pacific, accepted a position on Lou Holtz's staff at the University of Arkansas and convinced Coach Holtz to bring me on as a graduate assistant. For me, this was a jump into big-time college football that would have a profound impact on my coaching career.

The next six years were a whirlwind tour through the world of college football. A series of great jobs and opportunities took Glena, our young family, and me all over the country. From Arkansas to Iowa State to Ohio State to North Carolina State and back to Pacific, it was a process of gaining invaluable experiences and developing a network in coaching that reached well beyond my years.

Head coaches Lou Holtz, Earle Bruce, and Monte Kiffin, along with a number of assistant coaches who would eventually go on to have exceptional coaching careers, would each play their own part in influencing my young coaching career. They all had strong personalities and were great thinkers. In these guys I saw different philosophies and approaches on how to coach and lead a team. Each of them had their own unique style, and they all had a special effect on their programs.

During those years, and even later when I had the opportunity to coach for various NFL teams, I was fortunate to work with coaches whose brilliance, insight, or personal style translated into a level of performance that seemed more like magic.

One of the coaches I'm most proud to say I worked under was Bud Grant with the Minnesota Vikings. Coach Grant is the third-winningest professional football coach in history, with a combined 290 victories in the National and Canadian Football Leagues, in addition to having successful playing careers in the NFL, CFL, *and* NBA. His record is beyond legendary, but having seen him work up close, I can say that it was his intuitive powers that truly amazed me and I remain in awe of those abilities to this day. He saw what was happening in front of him so much more clearly than anyone else. Like other great sports figures, such as Muhammad Ali and Joe Namath, it seemed that just by making a prediction Coach Grant could make it come to life.

I recall one such story when we were playing our season opener against the San Francisco 49ers. They had just won the Super Bowl the previous year and were obviously an intimidating opponent for us. The night before the game, Coach Grant gathered us all together and gave a short, simple speech. In essence, he told us that the Niners were used to winning easy. Their strength, he told us, would be their weakness. They had so much offense and had been so productive when it came to scoring that they were simply not accustomed to being in a close game.

"If we can keep the game close," Coach Grant told us, "we'll beat these guys in the fourth quarter. They'll tighten up, they'll have problems, and they won't know what to do with the situation."

Sure enough, the fourth quarter came around and we had managed to keep the game close, being down only 28–21. We had just scored but needed another possession to at least tie the game, but time was running out. The stadium was roaring, and I was listening on the headset when Coach Grant called the kickoff team together. "Kick it to number twenty-six," he told them confidently. "Kick it to twenty-six, he'll fumble it."

Sounds impossible, right? How could anyone know such a thing? But sure enough, our kicker sent the ball to number twenty-six, he fumbled the ball when he got hit by one of our players, and we recovered it at the fifty-yard line. It was unbelievable. Everyone went berserk except Bud, who just stood there with a satisfied smile on his face, as calm as ever. Coach Grant just had that way about him. I was beginning to see how the true power of positive attitudes and clear intentions could affect outcomes.

Of all the great coaches I have worked with, none would have a more fundamental impact on the tactical side of my coaching than Monte Kiffin.

Besides being the preeminent defensive expert in modern-day football, he has been a generous friend. Monte has provided me with what seems like a lifetime of advice, opportunity, and mentoring, and certainly plenty of laughs both inside and outside the game of football. We've been sharing information and having conversations since we were first introduced to each other at the University of

Arkansas in 1977, where he served as the defensive coordinator. Certainly, the hallmarks of Monte's aggressive, attacking style defense can be found in the defenses I have coordinated over the years. His trademark "Tampa 2" defense is legendary in football circles and has definitely been a factor in many of our wins.

Monte is a tactical genius who has been a great influence on my defensive game over the years. His greatest contribution to my career, however, came early on—long before I ever entered the NFL—when he impressed upon me a simple but powerful belief: *In order to be successful, you must have a consistent philosophy. If you change who you are from year to year,* he explained, *you're never going to be great at anything.* I remember vividly when Monte pulled out a sheet of paper, which had no more than five or six sentences on it, and shared his philosophy. The essence of his philosophy was crystal clear: For him, it came down to playing with great effort and great discipline. Everything else flowed from that.

At the time, I was amazed at how clearly and succinctly he was able to express his philosophy. This was something I had never really seen another coach do. It was an inspiring and humbling moment in my development as a coach. For the first time, I saw the importance of being able to organize your thoughts and feelings about your work. At some point, I realized, I was going to have to stop just collecting pieces and develop a philosophy of my own.

It never dawned on me to take the time to reflect and evaluate what each learning experience meant—not just as an idea, but in terms of my entire journey, past, present, and future. From Redwood High School to the cusp of the NFL, I had been making great strides, but I now realize that in a sense I had also been doing exactly the opposite of what Monte was suggesting.

I had been operating with a multitude of ideas without a comprehensive philosophy to bring them all together. It would still be a long time before that afternoon at home when I finally pulled out a pen and paper and started writing. The realization that I would need to have a philosophy in order to really maximize my potential was one of the breakthrough moments in my personal education and professional career.

3

THE INNER GAME OF FOOTBALL

In my early years as a coach I was influenced by Abraham Maslow, Tim Gallwey, and Michael Murphy. Each had a profound impact on my learning and eventual teaching. Yet as the years passed, Gallwey's "Inner Game" concept proved to be the most influential. The essence of the Inner Game is to acquire and maintain a "quieted mind," which may then allow an athlete to perform at his or her highest level. Most of my coaching has revolved around enabling players and teams to achieve this state of mind.

The only competition that matters is the one that takes place within yourself. It isn't about external factors. Tim Gallwey and his Inner Game approach to performance has had a huge impact on how I look at the challenges of coaching. Specifically, Gallwey wrote about how human beings tend to enter a state of doubt when faced with the unknown or uncertainty. When that occurs, he wrote, we instinctively "overtighten." Physically, when we doubt our ability, we will tend to overtighten our muscles. Mentally, we fear failure and can become emotional and distracted.

This seemed so obvious when I read it, but until Gallwey, nobody had pointed it out. Examples I immediately thought of were about a basketball player failing to follow through when shooting a timely three-pointer, or a wide receiver short-arming a pass across the middle when he senses a safety bearing down on him. Gallwey's illustration of overtightening was a golfer who doubts his ability on a short putt; he tenses up as he makes contact with the golf ball, and misses a shot he could have made if only he had been playing loose.

Gallwey says that the concept of overtightening is nearly a "universal principle," and it certainly happens in football. Like any other sport, football presents physical and mental challenges. It is our job as coaches to prepare players in every regard possible. When players know that they have mastered the rigors of training, whether on the football field or in the weight room or classroom, then their confidence leads to an unusual focus, free from distractions, doubt, or fear. This attentiveness, also known as a quieted mind, clears the way for athletes to perform to their highest potential.

Think of young children playing. They don't worry about being judged, and they are only concerned with having fun. In those moments, it's easy to observe true, uninhibited play. We witness a level of concentration where the children are totally immersed, unaware of the world around them. This fascination and ability to be supremely focused are essential for their development, much like an athlete.

An athlete's immersion in and focus on performance allows for a lost sense of time in much the same way. When we have confidence and allow ourselves to become fascinated, the world seems to move in slow motion. It is an altered state of consciousness that comes from an extreme level of focus. Some performers describe this as resembling an out-of-body experience.

One of the first times such a moment happened to me was in

the batter's box at a northern California high school baseball field in the spring of 1968. We were having a disastrous game against the league leader, and I was at bat in the final inning. As I stepped up to the plate, an odd thought came into my mind: *Whatever you do right now, there's no way you're going to change the outcome of this game.* A pessimistic thought, sure, but instead of depressing me, it was liberating.

As I settled into the batter's box and prepared for the first pitch, everything seemed normal—until the pitcher, a gifted athlete who was known as "Big Mike," began his windup. I remember it like it was yesterday. He'd been pitching a spectacular game, and as he shifted his weight, brought up his arms, and lifted his left leg off the mound, his form was picture perfect, just as it had been all night, with one important difference: Mike seemed to be moving in slow motion. His hand released one of the most perfect-looking sliders I had ever seen, and everything seemed like it was taking forever. As the baseball hurtled toward me, it appeared to be rotating so slowly that I swear I could have counted the stitches. Even before I started my swing, there was no doubt in my mind that I was going to clobber it, and sure enough, the ball came off the bat with a sweetness that was nothing short of dreamlike. The ball flew straight over the pitcher's head, then the center fielder's head for an inside-the-park home run.

The point here isn't that I was liberated by the fact that my team's situation was hopeless but rather that I was freed up because I wasn't worried about the outcome. All I had to do was "let it happen," just watch the ball, and swing the bat, with nothing else going through my mind. As expected, that great shot didn't change the outcome of the game, but it was the slow-motion magic of that homer, and not the final score, that has stayed with me for all this time. In that moment, I had the experience of fully being a natural, instinctive athlete, without concerns or worries.

That is the mentality that we, as coaches, want to re-create for our players.

We want our players to be free of distractions and totally absorbed, ideally just like a child, fascinated with the game itself and not necessarily the outcome.

One of my most vivid illustrations of the Inner Game in football was back in 1997. It was late in my first season in New England, and we had barely survived some staggering ups and downs. Jacksonville was next up on our schedule, and they had been on a tear, particularly at home, where they had won thirteen games in a row. My team was battered after losing our top running back, Curtis Martin, our top receiver, Terry Glenn, and our top defensive lineman, Willie McGinest, to injuries. Our chances of repeating as division champions, let alone making it to the play-offs, looked slim. We needed this game to stay alive in the race, and all the odds seemed stacked against us. Jacksonville's fans were notorious for being loud and raucous, creating a definite home-field advantage, and they had thirteen straight wins at home to prove it.

It was Saturday night at the hotel in Jacksonville, an hour before our last team meeting prior to Sunday's game. I was racking my brain for some pearls of wisdom that might give us an edge as we approached this daunting challenge. I have always valued this meeting as my final chance to impact the players. The tone would vary depending on the circumstances we were facing and what I thought the team needed to hear. In the case of Jacksonville, I wanted to neutralize everyone's concern about their home-field advantage. We needed to enter the game with a single shared mind-set. It was a real competitive challenge, with the local and national media absolutely convinced that Jacksonville was going to win.

Realizing we had a great challenge ahead of us, I went back to the principles of the Inner Game and decided to introduce the players to the concept of creating peak experiences, or playing in "the zone." I also pulled out a favorite teaching approach of mine, the Socratic method, where you enlist participation from your students by asking questions to the entire group. I asked if anybody in the room had ever pitched a perfect game or a no-hitter. I had already confirmed that strong safety Lawyer Milloy had done so in high school. Sure enough, Lawyer took the bait, raised his hand, and told us all about it. I made sure he told us about what it felt like, in great detail. He remembered feeling "invincible," and I made him describe it. He had never felt so "powerful" and in such "total command" of a game as he had felt on that day. Of course, he was proudly telling us about his conquest, and we were amused with his story and delivery, as the seed had been planted. I asked others to share events in their background where they had felt similar sensations of extraordinary powers and invincibility.

Quarterback Drew Bledsoe told a story of his feelings prior to the Patriots' game against the San Diego Chargers in 1996. He told us that he saw the game in his mind before it happened. He knew that he would play one of his best games ever and that the Patriots would roll over the Chargers. As he played in the absence of fear, he felt that supreme confidence, and knew that he would perform extremely well. He did just that.

As the stories flowed, the energy of the night was well in order. The beauty of the Socratic method is that as you pose a question to the group and pause to call for a response, everybody in the room is thinking of an answer. They were all recalling their most perfect moments in sports, what we referred to as "peak experiences." I took the opportunity to define "peak experiences" and used the phrase "being in the zone." The team was collectively sharing thoughts of their most memorable peak experiences, and everybody seemed to be engaged. I made sure everyone in the room had an idea of what we were talking about, fielding questions and observations. When I felt we had come to something of a common understanding of "the zone," I posed another question. I asked the team, "Do you realize that every time you take the field you have an opportunity for a peak experience?" I told them that the zone doesn't have to be something that just mysteriously happens and that, with the right collective mind-set, we had the opportunity to create our own zone in our very next game.

First and foremost, we had to know that we were capable of winning this game. If there was any question, we were probably going to wind up as Jacksonville's fourteenth home win in a row. It was everybody's job to get his mind right by game time. I reminded them of all the ways we were going to outplay the Jaguars. It was their job to first believe it and then go out and execute the plan precisely. If they could ultimately trust in their ability to win, they could take the field with the "knowing" that would allow us to play instinctively with supreme confidence.

Second, we had to find total focus in the midst of one of the most difficult settings in the NFL. I directed them to acknowledge that the field would be the same size as always, 100 yards long and 53⅓ yards wide, with two end zones, twenty-two players, seven officials, four quarters, a normal halftime, and sixty minutes to play the game. The only difference from playing at our home stadium would be the decibel level of the Jaguars' loyal following. And it was going to be extremely loud. So in reality, the only thing that was going to challenge our ability to totally focus was the potential distraction of the noise, which might affect our communications and our ability to concentrate. Earlier in the year, at Buffalo, we had established a way to quiet an otherwise hostile crowd. We played well early and gave the Bills fans nothing to cheer about. We won 31–10. I reminded the team that the only thing we wanted to hear was the silence of the crowd.

The meeting had created a great feeling. The players had connected with one another by sharing their stories and baring their souls. They also had fun contributing to one of those special meetings that teams sometimes experience. So the scenario could be summed up simply: We needed to trust, we needed to focus, and we needed to get off to a good start by playing well early. I ended the meeting by focusing our attention past the outcome of the game. I proclaimed that someone was going to experience the zone on Sunday and that the weekend would not officially be over until we returned home with a win, and with one of them sharing their zone experience at the Monday morning meeting in Foxborough. All we had to do now was play the game.

Everything went well leading up to the game, and the stage was set. At kickoff, the crowd was crazed, the air was perfect, our will was strong, and our hopes were high. We didn't know it yet, but we were just about to witness one of the best starts to a game we could have imagined. A common assumption is that rookies don't always pay attention in meetings, especially toward the end of the season, but our rookie linebacker from Florida State, Vernon Crawford, was not only attentive that Saturday night, he took our message to the field on the very first play of the game.

Jacksonville won the coin toss, and we were poised to kick off. Our kickoff team, like others in the NFL, was basically manned by young, inexperienced players. This was a typical bunch of half-crazed headhunters hoping to do the right thing but always fearing they were just about to screw it all up. Vernon was about to become an instant hero, at least in my book. As our kick-off team raced down the field, Jacksonville's returner started to turn up into the left side of our coverage team, only to run head-on into Vernon Crawford. What resulted was a colossal hit that sent the football rocketing skyward. Vernon had made the hit of his life and forced a fumble on the opening kickoff of a huge game. A scramble for the football ensued, and we recovered it! The referee had barely signaled our recovery of the ball when Vernon Crawford came sprinting off the field screaming, "I'm in the zone! I'm in the zone! I'm in the zone!" Vernon really was paying attention!

The game started on the highest of notes and continued to crescendo from there. We delivered a tremendous upset, considering the circumstances. On that day we were invincible, and we performed with great precision and power. We played like we were in the zone, and the feeling affected us throughout the remainder of the schedule. One of my favorite sayings comes from the famous coach Lou Holtz. He preached that "the best players don't always win, but those that play the best most always do!" This certainly held true for the Patriots on that Sunday in Jacksonville, Florida. It fueled a very strong finish to an AFC Eastern Division Championship season that didn't end until the second round of the 1997 play-offs.

This may be my single best example of using the Inner Game concept in a team setting before a game. However, it is certainly not the only time I have used the concepts of total focus and supreme confidence to boost performance. It is a supremely confident athlete who will have the best chance to perform up to his or her potential.

With that in mind, I have always felt it is my duty to show my players exactly how they can develop their confidence. They have to prepare in a manner that will promote their skills. They have to be in great condition in all areas. They have to know the responsibilities of their positions. They have to know how they fit into the overall scheme of the team's design. Basically, they should leave no stone unturned in terms of preparation and readiness. All of these factors contribute to an athlete's feeling of supreme confidence and the ability to perform with a "quieted mind."

It has been an ongoing pursuit of mine to weave the principles of the Inner Game into developing individual and team performance.

4

HARD LESSONS IN NEW YORK

In my early years coaching in the NFL I made a lot of stops. I coached defense for several teams, and loved it. After coaching the defensive backs in Buffalo, I went to Minnesota to do the same under Coach Bud Grant, whose example taught me more about the art of coaching, leadership, and the importance of observing human behavior than any graduate class ever could. I loved everything about the coaching life—the strategy, the tactics, the focus, and the pace. I loved the tight-knit intensity of coaching a position group, and in my close relationship with the guys I coached, I guess I developed—for better or worse—a reputation for being a "player's coach."

Not everyone saw that as a positive, but I always felt it was important to have a relationship with the players I coached.

In 1990, I left Minnesota to take the defensive coordinator position with the New York Jets. While that job brought a new level of responsibility and pressure, I approached it with the same spirit I had approached every other opportunity in my career. We worked as hard and competed as much as we possibly could, and felt grateful to have the chance to do it.

After my second season with the Jets, I had the chance to interview for the Vikings' head coaching job. Though I didn't get it, I came to realize that as much as I loved coaching defense, I ultimately wanted to be a head coach. I now had a new goal, and my chance to test how ready I was came sooner than I could have guessed. We went 8–8 during our fourth season in New York and our head coach, Bruce Coslet, was let go. I had assumed that the team would mount a national search, but to my surprise that's not what happened. Instead, I was called in for a two-hour interview with the Jets general manager, Dick Steinberg. Soon after, the team offered me the head coaching position. It was exactly twenty years into my coaching career.

While being a head coach is certainly challenging and an unstable profession, it is also one that many people dream of. Twenty years into my coaching career I had my first opportunity to interview for a head coaching job, and while I knew it would be challenging, I was very excited to lead an organization. So when, at forty-three years old, I was offered the head coaching job with the New York Jets, I took it and wanted to have fun doing it. I felt I had a great advantage because I had already been with the team for four years. It was a team that I believed in, and while we were certainly going to have a tough fight ahead of us, I felt the team was ready, and I couldn't wait to put my ideas into practice.

I was coming into the job knowing the team had a clear sense of my style. I had had a lot of success coordinating the Jets' defense, and overall I felt accepted by the group.

I remember my first team meeting as the new head coach at the Jets. We were facing a difficult situation on a number of levels, and my first priority was adjusting the culture of the team. Officially, I was addressing the players, but essentially the entire organization was there: the coaching staff, the management, and even the team's owner, eighty-year-old self-made oil billionaire Leon Hess. The meeting room itself was familiar, but when you're a head coach everything changes, and I think everyone was wondering how different I would be from the Pete they had worked with in the past. I wanted to show them that they were going to get the same coach they had had the past four seasons—someone who was positive, focused, and extremely competitive. I believed that the only way we were going to succeed was as a single, united team.

As far as I was concerned, the success I'd had in the past with that approach was what had gotten me the head coaching job in the first place, and I didn't see any reason to change something that was working. The last thing in the world I wanted to do was throw away the things I had learned over the course of my career and pretend to be someone I wasn't. Walking into the meeting, I was determined that I was not going to transform into an unapproachable head coach. I was going to be me, no matter what.

The task of turning the Jets around was a serious undertaking, but I made every effort to keep the tone positive. The vision I wanted the team and staff to share wasn't about "not failing" but about really searching within yourself and developing a positive approach to winning. I wanted every member of the team to think of himself as a piece of our success. As I described how I saw our new competitive philosophy, the players and coaches began to buy in and seemed willing to at least give it a try. I was very pleased to watch the players, coaches, and staff members light up. They got it. They were on board. Well, most of them.

Leon Hess, the owner of the team and the man who signed my check, said nothing. It was clear from his expression that he was not a fan of the somewhat unorthodox approach I took. I respected him and his outlook, but in retrospect, I guess I wasn't his vision of an NFL head coach. While this bothered me to some degree, I told myself that I couldn't control how he felt, and I knew that I surely was not going to be successful by altering my approach. The tension was unfortunate, but I really didn't feel that I had a choice.

Unfortunately, after that first team meeting, Leon and I would not speak for the remainder of the season. In this initial meeting, I could have tempered my enthusiasm and considered my audience more closely, but I was too pumped. I wanted to get the message out—and my focus was on the players with whom I had spent the previous four seasons.

The players knew that I was passionate about the game of football. They had seen me use a variety of methods to get their attention and inspire them to work hard. I had already done a lot of crazy stuff to get my players jacked up, and one example was the legend of "the Beaver."

The Beaver saga actually started back when I was at Minnesota, with the help of my friend and Viking colleague Paul Wiggin. Paul was a longtime NFL player, former head coach at Stanford University and the Kansas City Chiefs, and a great coach. We were like the Odd Couple, with Paul playing Felix and me in the role of Oscar; he was keeping everything clean and I was messing everything up. We spent a great deal of time together, and of course we shared stories about working for other teams.

Late one night at the office, Paul told me how, when he'd been in charge of the service teams as an assistant coach at the 49ers, he used to give out an award to the player who practiced the hardest. It was such a small thing that it was almost silly. The player who worked the hardest earned the title of "eager Beaver." We laughed about it, but I listened when Paul told me that he'd gotten some really positive results with his gimmick. He had brought

it up as a funny story, but I saw it as another possible way to create a competitive environment. It was a lesson I was careful not to
forget.

When I left Minnesota to go to the Jets as defensive coordinator, one of my highest priorities was coming up with a way to emphasize the importance of forcing turnovers, and after giving it
some thought I decided to take a page from Paul's book and institute my own award, Beaver of the Week. We started with the lesson that the beaver is the most diligent worker in the animal
kingdom, and the player who was able to force the first fumble
that was recovered by us would earn the Beaver of the Week award.
We found a stuffed toy beaver that we put in the winner's locker
each week. Like Paul's version of the contest, it was no big deal, but
it stuck. And over time, the Beaver took on a life of its own. Somehow, part of the lore was that no one was allowed to talk about the
Beaver outside of our meeting room. We would never talk to the
media about it, never speak about what it was. We made it our little secret. The media suspected there was something about a beaver,
but no one would ever tell them. I think that secrecy was actually
part of what made it work so well. The Beaver gave our guys something to compete for, and it also gave us a common experience that
no one outside our circle could share. It really was the best of both
worlds.

Ultimately, the Beaver phenomenon outgrew the locker room,
and it got so big that it followed us everywhere we went. Each game,
after the first fumble recovery, it would get tossed onto the field—
which was totally illegal, of course. And all of a sudden a second
competition evolved, as we had to get the Beaver off the field before
the referees spotted it. This wasn't always as easy as it sounds.

We were playing the Patriots in New England and had just forced
a fumble during the first quarter. Greg Robinson, one of our defen-

sive coaches at the time, had the Beaver on a rope hanging from his belt, and in an excess of enthusiasm he threw it out there a little too far—and it landed right at the feet of a referee on national television! The poor official couldn't figure out whether to throw a penalty or not, and the legend of the Beaver grew.

It was a little thing, but it helped keep us focused on what I had decided was important to our success. In this case it was turnovers, but it could have been anything. What mattered was that we did everything in our power to focus the players on our priority and have them buy into it without worrying whether it was silly or not. I think anyone who was on the team back then would tell you that it was more than just a fun distraction; it helped us play better football.

Even though we were developing an unconventional approach, I believed that these shared experiences built trust within our team, an essential part of being successful. I wanted the coaches and players to know that I had the utmost confidence in them, so they could work hard and enjoy the ride. This laid the foundation for what I thought I needed to succeed as a head coach.

After the annual NFL draft and our fall training camp, it was finally time for our first game of the season, and it was one to remember. The date was Sunday, September 4, 1994, and my first game as a head coach of the New York Jets was against the Buffalo Bills. The Bills were then coached by the great Marv Levy, and they had a roster full of Pro Bowl players, such as Jim Kelly, Thurman Thomas, Andre Reed, and Bruce Smith. They had been winning for years and had just appeared in four straight Super Bowls. Their organization set the bar in the league, and their "K-Gun" offense was as difficult to defend against as any offense I had ever seen.

We were in a rebuilding mode in New York, trying to put together something that would give us some substance and momentum. We beat the Bills that day 23–3. It was a huge victory and a great moment for us. After the game, I was on cloud nine. I was 1-0 as a head coach and confidant that we would have a winning season.

That night after the game, like I've done on many occasions, I went back into the stadium. When the crowds are gone, and the only people around are the guys sweeping up, there's a special quiet in the air that speaks to me in a way that nothing else does. That's exactly what I did on this occasion—I was hoping to hang on to such a great feeling just a little bit longer.

After a couple of minutes, I turned to walk back toward our team buses. I noticed for the first time all of Buffalo's division championship banners on display—and it dawned on me that, while we had just won a great game, since Coach Levy had been there, they had put up winning season after winning season, division championship after division championship. There must have been six or seven of them up there. And as I stood there congratulating myself on my brand-new 1-0 record as an NFL head coach, it hit me: *Now that's success.* Those guys had shown that they had what it took to continue to win year after year, in an almost permanent state of winning.

It would be years before the phrase "Win Forever" formed as a philosophy for me, but from that day forward, the image of those championship banners lined up one next to the other at Rich Stadium was fixed in my mind. During my time with the Jets, the San Francisco 49ers, and later the New England Patriots, I kept returning to that moment. It was something I knew was important, although at the time I couldn't quite put it in its place.

After that first game, our season continued to be promising. Our team had come together and we started 6-5 in the difficult AFC East. In many ways the season at that point actually seemed to be shaping up better than our record showed.

Then came the Miami game. We were playing at home for first place in the division against the Dolphins and Hall of Fame quarterback Dan Marino in front of the largest home crowd to date, 75,606. We were up 24–21 with twenty-two seconds left and Miami had the ball at our eight-yard line. With the clock winding down, Marino yelled, "Clock, clock!" signaling that he was about to spike the ball and thus stop the clock. Instead, Marino faked the spike and threw a beautiful fade route to Mark Ingram for a touchdown. "The fake spike" is justifiably remembered as one of the all-time great bait-and-switch plays in NFL history. It was also a devastating loss for our team, and we were never able to recover our momentum. We went on to lose our next four games to finish a once promising season 6-10.

As tough as it was for us, what really worried me were the decisions we were going to have to make in the off-season. The new salary cap had just gone into effect, and to make matters worse, a few of the veteran leaders on our team were approaching the end of their careers, and it was not likely that we were going to keep them.

As we were working our way through it early in the off-season, and as I was dreading a few of those personnel decisions, I soon found out that it would not be my problem.

Late one afternoon in early January, I was summoned to Dick Steinberg's office, a more or less daily occurrence in those days. Dick, the general manager at the time, had hired me for the head coaching job, and I knew he was as stressed out as I was about the future of our veterans and the direction of the organization. I also knew he believed there was a light at the end of the tunnel and trusted that we were on our way to getting there. I assumed this was another one of our many strategy sessions.

I walked across the hall into his office, and as I entered, Dick was sitting at his desk with his head down, avoiding eye contact with me. Right away, something didn't feel right, but I still had no idea what was up. Then, looking around, I saw Leon Hess sitting all the way across the room from Dick in a single chair, with another chair in front of him. Gesturing toward the chair, Leon said, "Pete, come over here and sit down."

I crossed the room and sat down, wondering what this was all about. True to form, Leon didn't waste any time getting to the point. "In the business world," he said, "a man in your situation would resign. But I know you're not going to do that, so I'm going to have to let you go."

I was caught completely off guard and couldn't believe my ears.

A man in my situation?

Was he serious? I had been in the job for less than a year, and here I was being blindsided! I couldn't think of how to respond, but it was clear that nothing I said would make any difference at this point. All I could see in Leon's eyes was that he had made up his mind.

At first I was in total disbelief.

My very next thought was, *This might be the best thing that ever happened to me.* After all, I had a four-year contract with three more years left on it, and this guy was letting me go. Rebuilding a team with an owner who doesn't see eye to eye with you is an uphill battle in the best of circumstances, and while I was looking forward to the challenge, there was no question that it would have been incredibly tough to pull off. Moments earlier I had been full of dread about what the next season would hold, and all of a sudden everything had changed. In any case, there wasn't any point in arguing.

I didn't say anything. I just walked out. Later I heard that he had made the decision to get rid of me after learning that Rich Kotite had been fired from the Philadelphia Eagles and would be available to step in. Personally, though, I think he had more or less made up his mind during that first team meeting, considering we never spoke one time during the entire season. In that first meeting, I think he came to the conclusion that I was somehow not right for the situation, or possibly not serious enough, to be the head coach his organization needed.

At the press conference when he announced the change, Leon Hess put on a big smile for the occasion. "I'm eighty years old," he told the reporters. "I want results now, not five years from now." Fair enough, but unfortunately for everyone involved, results were exactly what he got—dramatic results, just not the ones he wanted. The Jets went 4-28 for the next two seasons, after which Kotite was unceremoniously fired as well.

And where was I during that press conference? After I walked out of Dick's office, I rounded up my wife and kids, and within days we were on our way to Disney World, obviously seeking a drastic change of scenery.

Was Leon wrong to fire me? Maybe he was and maybe he wasn't. It was his team, and he had the right to do whatever he wanted with it. A more interesting question is whether he made that decision because of *what* I was doing or because of *how* I was doing it. If I am being completely honest, I would have to say that it probably was a bit of both. I was new in the role of head coach and did not have my act completely together. That said, I still think that we were on the right track, and I wish I could have seen how it all would have played out, given more time.

In the long run, I have to admit that I probably contributed to my firing by the Jets because I didn't do everything I could have done to make sure the owner understood my vision. Looking back, I didn't understand the scope of my approach well enough to explain it to him in a convincing way. I mistakenly thought that having the team's attention was enough. I still had some work to do when it came to defining and articulating my philosophy.

5

THE 49ERS WAY

In the ensuing weeks, I would take some comfort from still being under contract and having the breathing room to weigh my options. As other NFL jobs opened up, though, I quickly began to feel the urge to return to the field. After all, I had barely gotten a chance to get started at the Jets, and I was ready for more. I was still confident I was going to be a successful head coach if given the right opportunity. But realistically, I needed to set my sights on a defensive coordinator position.

Unfortunately, the window for coaching jobs in the NFL is small and closes almost as quickly as it opens. It is just the nature of the beast. You have to be ready to jump on something the moment it comes along, or more than likely you will miss your shot. As a professional coach, you are prepared for that. Where things get tricky is when several opportunities come up at once. As I was looking into which NFL coordinator jobs were about to open, I received a telephone call from Mike Shanahan, the new head coach at the Denver Broncos. They were preparing to hire a defensive coordinator, and he wanted me to come out to Denver to interview for the position. Mike wanted to build a whole new defensive staff. Despite a 7-9 record that year—thanks in large part to great performances by quarterback John Elway—they had probably been the worst team in the league defensively. This made the coordinator job a very exciting prospect.

In a lot of ways it would be a solid situation for me. Given the Broncos' previous performance, it seemed clear that there would be virtually no expectations of me in the short term and yet a huge potential upside if the defense could be built to complement Elway and the offense. I could have a strong hand in the rebuilding, and it was hard to see how anything would not be an improvement over what had come before. Besides, I had already gotten myself into a rebuilding frame of mind before I had unexpectedly been let go from the Jets.

This seemed to be exactly what I needed after leaving New York. Mike was an excellent coach, and he was coming from San Francisco, where he had been the offensive coordinator under George Seifert, whom I respected and admired enormously. I knew he would be bringing with him a style and mentality that I understood and respected. As I hung up the phone after agreeing to fly out the next day, the only question in my mind was whether or not I'd be offered the job.

The next day as I was getting ready to leave for the airport, the phone rang again. On the line this time was Coach Seifert. The 49ers had just won the Super Bowl 49–26 over the San Diego Chargers, and George was on his way down to Los Angeles to tape *The Tonight Show*. He had a bombshell to drop on me. The news hadn't been made public yet, but Ray Rhodes, George's defensive coordinator, had been offered the head job with the Philadelphia Eagles and was going to take it. And so, with my suitcase literally packed for Denver, George had called to ask if I would be interested in coming out there to talk about replacing Ray—and he wanted me to come *that day*. As exciting as it sounded, and though San Francisco was my home-town, I felt that I had made at least some degree of commitment to talk to Mike first. My initial response was to explain the situation to George and say, "Sorry, I'm gonna go to Denver and do the right thing."

Besides, I told myself after I had put down the phone, Denver was clearly the smart move for me. An hour earlier it hadn't even been a question. Yet now something deep inside me suddenly didn't feel quite right. The fact that Mike was coming from George's 49ers was one of the selling points for Denver, and here I was turning down George himself without even so much as an interview. Halfway to the airport, I had the taxicab pull over at a pay phone on the side of the Long Island Expressway where I called George back. We agreed that I would go to Denver first and then come see him the next day.

I ended up being offered both jobs, which forced me to take a long, hard look in the mirror.

In one regard, the Denver job would be somewhat easier because expectations were lower, and it was a great opportunity to advance my career and reputation. Going to San Francisco meant following a Super Bowl season that would leave me facing incredibly high expectations and also stepping into the shoes of a high-profile defensive coordinator in Ray Rhodes. Deep down, some part of me had to know that my heart was really in San Francisco, but on a pragmatic level I really just didn't feel that I could take it.

After meeting with George, I spent most of that night alone in my San Francisco hotel room, on the phone with my wife, Glena, trying to think it through. Finally she asked me the question I hadn't been able to ask myself: "Are you afraid the expectations are too high in San Francisco?"

And all of a sudden it clicked. What she was asking me was, *Were the expectations too big for me at the 49ers? Was I really not prepared to compete on that stage?* As soon as I came to terms with what my hesitation was actually all about, I called George and told him I would take the job if he still wanted me. Fortunately, he said yes.

Going to San Francisco turned out to be absolutely the right decision. As a kid growing up in the Bay Area, I had always been a huge 49ers fan, and their style and success were ones I always admired. As a graduate assistant and young college coach, I would return with my family to Marin County in the summers to visit my parents. Whenever I got the chance I would visit Coach Seifert, who was coaching the Niners' defensive backs at the time. George would let me sit in his office and ask questions about the NFL, the philosophy of former 49ers head coach Bill Walsh, and overall defense. It was in his office that I became familiar with professional football and the business behind the sport. When I had a chance to interview with NFL teams, I was fortunate to have had that behind-the-scenes experience. Without those sessions hanging out with George, I would in many ways have been starting from scratch when I moved from college coaching to NFL coaching. Thus, I was thrilled to have the chance to go back home and coordinate his defense.

The 49ers had been the team I had rooted for as a kid, and I was honored to coach for them and George. Being a defensive coach himself, he easily could have micromanaged me, but instead he allowed me to call the defense and have an ownership of our scheme. Along with that, we would often discuss how he managed his team and his staff in more general ways, as I was constantly thinking about how I would lead a team when given the chance again. I wanted to take every opportunity I could to learn from his recent success.

Coach Walsh was another great source of guidance and insight during this period. When I came aboard, the 49ers were coming off a Super Bowl victory and everything in the organization was clicking. Before my second season, Coach Walsh was hired as a consultant. I couldn't have been more excited because in addition to being one of the coaches I most admired, he also was one of the guests whom Professor Albaugh had brought into class when I was a graduate student at UOP, and just beginning to formulate my coaching style.

During my time with the Niners, I would often bounce between the staff room and Coach Bill McPherson's office, learning about the culture of the organization. Coach Mac coached linebackers and was a quiet legend during the years when the 49ers were a dominant team in the NFL. He was one of my closest friends on the staff. Coach Mac would always give me the viewpoint of an assistant coach experiencing the systems under Walsh and Seifert. He loved both coaches as leaders of the Niners, and he was able to describe and differentiate their unique and subtle nuances. He helped me to understand the essence of the Niners' culture.

It was very interesting to see how the assistants reacted when Coach Walsh entered the facility or a staff meeting. They had such a sense of respect for him and he was held in such high regard that they were nervous and on edge around him. Because of his intimidating presence, he was typically left alone for most of the day. Since I had not been there when he was leading the organization, I didn't feel that sense of protocol—and he certainly didn't insist on it. I was quite comfortable around him and stopped by whenever I could. In his office we would spend hours chatting and I would ask him a variety of questions about how he changed the culture of the Niners, including the details of his philosophy. For me, it was an incredible experience, as he was able to explain to me the spectrum of his approach, ranging from personnel decisions to coaching decisions and more.

We talked a lot about the quarterback position. Coach Walsh was one of the great quarterback gurus in the history of the game, and he convinced me that everything a coach does in designing his offense should be about making it easy for the quarterback, because his job is so difficult. He believed that everything should be structured with the quarterback in mind. We talked a lot about the discipline that was necessary to do this when designing game plans, structuring practices, and calling plays.

One time when we were talking, I asked Coach Walsh what he looked for in evaluating quarterbacks. If the entire offensive game revolved around the quarterback, what kind of player was he looking for? His answer was simple, a revelation. "All I'm looking for," Coach answered, "is a guy who can throw a catchable ball." He went on to talk about Joe Montana and said that what made him so special wasn't that he had the greatest arm in the game but that he could be relied upon to throw a ball that could be caught with near-total consistency. That's an incredibly rare thing in a player—and a totally unique insight by a coach. I still think about Coach Walsh's "catchable ball" today when I evaluate potential quarterbacks during recruiting, draft preparation, or free agency and have never forgotten the importance of building an offense that is focused on protecting the quarterback, first and foremost.

Coach Walsh and I also talked many times about eliminating doubt and how much easier it is to perform when you truly believe in your preparation. That led us to a discussion about preparation and practice.

Coach Walsh was a great believer in "contingency planning." His approach was that preparation and practice sessions should be designed so that the performer is trained for all potential outcomes and events. When you plan and train for all possible contingencies, you eliminate surprises and, in turn, eliminate a huge source of doubt that so often make us tighten up.

Coach Walsh applied the concept of contingency planning not just to practice but to all aspects of his program, including personnel, scouting, coaching, training, travel, teaching, public relations, and nutrition. In all areas, he wanted to have a plan for everything that could possibly happen. The basis for the philosophy was simple but brilliant—have a plan for all eventual outcomes, and you'll be prepared. To accomplish this, a coach must prepare a step-by-step approach that encompasses all possible results.

What I learned from Coach Walsh during my time with the 49ers was that this approach can apply to all facets of your personal life, as well as your working life. There is, however, another side to this; for better or worse, once you start down this path of contingency planning, the quest to cover all bases never ends. Once I accepted this line of thinking and incorporated it into my daily life, everything changed.

Often, when I left his office, I felt the same way I had with Coach Grant in Minnesota: privileged to pick the brain of one of the great minds in my profession. It was as though Coach Walsh let me in on his professional secrets. By the time I left the 49ers for the Patriots, I felt I really understood the reasons behind the San Francisco 49ers' profound success. Because Coach Walsh was so open to share his insights and so generous with his time, I felt that I understood it in a way that was available to few outside—or even inside—the organization.

The following year when I was interviewing for the head coaching job in New England, those sessions with Coach Walsh were invaluable. I had gained so many insights into what it took to run an organization, not only from Coach Walsh, but from Coach Seifert as well. I had learned that they were winners not solely because of their win/loss records but also because of their strict attention to detail, confidence in themselves, and rock solid philosophies.

My time at the 49ers was a great experience for me. Working so closely with Coach Seifert supported the strong views on defense that I already held, and my time with both him and Coach Walsh provided me with a wealth of new insights into what it took to succeed as a head coach—in the NFL or anywhere.

6

GETTING CLOSER IN NEW ENGLAND

At the end of my second season with the 49ers, George Seifert decided to step down, and I felt that it was time for me to move on as well. The head coaching position at the St. Louis Rams opened up, and I was asked to interview. The interview went well, but when they asked if I could commit to taking the job if it was offered, I wasn't prepared to do that. I had a feeling that something else might come up, and I needed to wait and see how it might unfold. The New England Patriots' head coaching position was open, and they pursued George first, because their owner really wanted the San Francisco system. When he couldn't get George, I became a candidate, and I will always be grateful to George for setting that up for me.

When I was offered the job in New England, the owner, Robert Kraft, told me, "We want it to be just like the 49ers." That was music to my ears. Whether it was office dynamics, travel arrangements, or schematics of their offense and defense—everything the 49ers did was first-class and professional. They were consistently efficient and effective in every aspect of their team. I wanted any organization I led to have those qualities as well. After thinking about the St. Louis and New England opportunities, it became clear once again that I desired the more competitive situation. After just two years, with great fortune and backing from the 49ers, I was a head coach again in the National Football League.

When I entered the Patriots' facility for the first time as their head coach, I was full of optimism. I was getting the chance to build my own team based on the successful principles I had learned in San Francisco. I had been brought on to do this, and I couldn't wait to get started. Unfortunately, it took only a couple of weeks for me to realize that the front office and I did not agree philosophically on many important fronts. They had a culture in place that was different from mine, and they were highly skeptical of embracing wholesale change. While they wanted to resemble the 49ers, they were very comfortable with certain aspects of their organization, and rightfully so, as they had been AFC champions the previous year. I was about to learn an important lesson about the difficulty of implementing change in an established organization.

I remember calling Coach Seifert and Coach Walsh early on to tell them how the Patriot organization was resisting the way I wanted to do things. I asked their advice on what would be the most effective response from me. Coach Seifert was specifically adamant that I not change who I was or my mentality. He said clearly, "Pete, you've got to do it the way you know how to." After my experience in New York, I wondered if I shouldn't try to be more political, but the advice I got from these two mentors was uncompromising—and some of the best I ever received. If I began to try to please others by changing, I would be miserable. That support was incredibly important and helped get me through the challenging early days with the organization.

After hearing that advice I decided to trust my instincts and compete to be the best head coach I knew how to be.

Our roster was loaded with great competitors and incredible

athletes. Outstanding players like Curtis Martin, Willie McGinest, Ted Johnson, and Drew Bledsoe, as well as unique role players like Troy Brown and Tedy Bruschi, among others, made this a championship team.

A great young player on this team who was emerging as a leader and a true tough guy was safety Lawyer Milloy. He was fiery and loaded with classic football savvy and instincts. Early on we targeted him as a guy who could influence others—he was a player teammates would be quick to follow. Whenever we found a player like this, we worked to display and utilize his unique qualities to the fullest. I always believed that it was important to demonstrate to your team your willingness to highlight special talents. When we positioned Lawyer to take advantage of his toughness and playmaking ability, he quickly became a huge factor on our defense.

Tedy Bruschi was another player whose extraordinary talents had not yet fully come to light. Tedy was one of the all-time best pass rushers in the history of college football, but his undersized stature and style had limited his opportunities as a starter. As our staff got to know Tedy and realized what an incredible competitor he was, we knew we had to find a starting position and a larger role for him. So Tedy became a starting weak-side linebacker and a specialty pass rusher. He would play a huge role on the team in the upcoming years. I've always tried to uncover special qualities in players and build roles and styles that make the most of their unique talents.

Our first season was a blast. We had a great time as we competed week in and week out throughout that season. We were AFC East champions and made it to the second round of the 1997 play-offs, where the Pittsburgh Steelers beat us 7–6. While the loss was a difficult one to stomach, I was still energized for the next season.

A major reason I felt so optimistic at the end of my first year in New England was the way the season had unfolded for our quarterback, Drew Bledsoe. When I got there, the team was just coming off a loss in the Super Bowl to the Green Bay Packers. There was enormous pressure on Drew. The story line in the New England press leading up to the Super Bowl had been, more or less, "If Bledsoe plays well, the Pats will win, and if he doesn't, the Pats will lose." After they lost, Drew caught a fair amount of heat, and it was still an issue when I took over as head coach.

Coming out of college as the number one overall NFL draft pick, Drew was expected not only to perform well but also to slide easily into the leadership role expected of a star quarterback. For all his ability and hard work, Drew was a quiet, fairly self-contained person. I think Drew's naturally reserved nature was at times considered by others to be a lack of fire or even an arrogance—which didn't help things at all with the notoriously tough New England media. I hadn't been there at the time, but I assumed that the staff had challenged Drew early on, to encourage his growth and maturity. While he did the work and generally played well, he may have felt a bit underappreciated on the team. At least, that was the way I sized up the situation.

Coming into the job, I thought the best thing that could ever happen would be to find a way to turn Drew's situation around. Even with his quiet ways, I believed Drew could be much more powerful if he could develop into more of a vocal leader as well as the star of the team.

So we worked to highlight the positive aspects of Drew's performance, especially where he was doing things his teammates could really appreciate—the extra effort, the great read, the great throw, getting pounded in the pocket and still making a good throw, getting up after being sacked and coming back on the next snap as if nothing had happened. These moments weren't hard to find. We decided to focus on all the good things he was doing.

As that first season progressed, we started to see some changes in Drew's role on the team. I felt confident in dealing with him, and as he matured he became increasingly willing to open up and embrace his role of a team leader. From time to time, I would remind him that it might be appropriate to say something in a team setting, and he would do it. At other times he would act on his own impulse. He seemed comfortable taking over, and it was a beautiful thing for our team. I can't take credit for all of this—part of it was simply the process of his maturing—but I truly believe the head coach can and should nurture potential leaders as they emerge.

Great leaders in sports seem to have a knack for creating defining moments, and that's exactly what Drew did in the fourth quarter of a pivotal game against Miami. What could have been a game-ending injury for Drew instead turned into one of those moments.

We were behind in the game but coming back strong until, after one play, Drew unexpectedly came out of the huddle and called time-out. I had no idea what was going on until he came to the sideline and told me that he couldn't feel one of his fingers. He wasn't sure if he could even hold on to the ball. The trainer took a look and thought Drew had broken his index finger.

It was terrible news for us, as our backup quarterback, Scott Zolak, had only played a handful of times that season. After a few moments, I decided that I would rather play Drew with an injured finger than with our backup. So I sent Drew back in, broken finger and all. With him in the game, I reasoned, we still had a chance. After powering through a few plays with time running out, it came down to a critical fourth-down situation, and Drew completed a beautiful pass to Shawn Jefferson on the sideline—just enough to get us that first down and keep us alive. I was thrilled, but then Drew called another unexpected time-out and jogged over to the sideline.

"Coach," he said, clearly upset. "This is crazy. I can't even control the ball!"

"What are you talking about?" I responded, thinking that he had just thrown a perfect pass and that this was not the time for a lack of confidence. "You just made a great throw." Drew gave me a look.

"Coach," he said, "I was trying to throw the ball to Ben!"

What I hadn't realized was that the pass that had hit Shawn Jefferson so perfectly on the sideline had actually been intended for the tight end—who had been in the center of the field! But I really still felt that Drew was the best chance we had, and in spite of his reservations, he went back in to finish the game, eventually throwing a winning touchdown pass to Terry Glenn (which, ironically enough, was intended for Shawn Jefferson).

That was the moment I had been waiting for. When it came out in the press that he had finished the game with a broken finger, Drew's status in New England seemed to elevate. New England is a really tough area to play in, but the fans and the press embraced him after that. It was really a big moment for him in terms of the outside world, and ultimately it cemented the positive developments he had been working on within the team.

Drew didn't stop being a quiet guy after that. That's just who he is. But people's sense of him changed, and they started seeing him for the leader he really was. I couldn't have made that happen in a million years on my own, but when that broken finger came along, Drew came through in heroic fashion.

Was Drew a great quarterback before he played through a broken finger? Of course he was. He was a natural leader as well, even if it wasn't obvious to everyone around him. As time went on it would continue to be important to promote Drew as the leader of our team.

Not every player had Drew's status or his star quality. Jimmy Hitchcock was a great example of this. Jimmy was a talented but undistinguished cornerback. When I arrived at the Patriots in 1997, I was told he had hit rock bottom with the coaches on the previous staff. A third-round draft pick out of the University of North Carolina in 1995, in his first professional season he had been an up-and-down player working to make his place as a regular contributor. He was somewhat erratic during his first few seasons. His ability was never the issue, for at times he performed like some of the best players in the game, but at others he could make some bonehead plays. By the time I arrived, Jimmy's previous coaches had run out of patience—and even worse, they had lost interest.

The year prior to my arrival Jimmy had not only had been benched but had actually been eliminated from the dress squad for games. As explained to me, Jimmy had not played well in games in spite of the fact that he had given full effort in practice and had studied his playbook. He was committed to giving it his all, but the harder he tried, the worse he played and the more trouble he encountered. His relationship with his coaches just seemed to worsen.

I was hoping that Jimmy's problem wasn't a matter of effort or ability but maybe just a loss of confidence. His former coaches were only willing to talk about his success in black-and-white terms of "getting it done." Thus, not only were they not solving his problem, but perhaps were only making it worse.

It seemed to be a classic example of self-fulfilling prophecy. While coaches openly and repeatedly challenged Jimmy in hopes of improving his play, he continued to struggle and eventually he was benched.

Both as a competitor and as a teacher, I believed that Jimmy's situation presented an opportunity for a new approach. In meeting with him, it was clear he felt defeated. His self-esteem was low and his confidence was shaken. With all of his strengths, Jimmy Hitch-cock really didn't know whether or not he had what it took to perform at the NFL level.

Because Jimmy was the kind of person who had tremendous pride and a real willingness to learn, we decided to address him only in a manner that supported what self-confidence he had left. We worked hard with Jimmy, and as part of our process we made sure we engineered opportunities that helped him succeed. Soon enough, we began to see results. Jimmy not only earned a starting spot in our first season in Foxborough but went on to lead the entire NFL in both interception return yards and defensive touchdowns in 1998. Head coaches encounter opportunities to affect their players' performances and it is their job to recognize them.

In our second year, I felt we had a chance to put together a good run if we could build off year one. As the season started, we were playing well on offense, with Drew leading the way again, and a sound defense was working aggressively to create turnovers. But not everything was working so smoothly, as we encountered issues along the way that would require special attention and eventually called for outside advice.

Terry Glenn was our star wide receiver and one of the most talented players I'd ever been around. He'd won the Biletnikoff Award as the nation's top receiver at Ohio State after walking on and left Columbus as the seventh overall player drafted in 1996 by New England. During his rookie season, he had ninety receptions for 1,132 yards while helping the Patriots get to the Super Bowl, but during the next few seasons he became inconsistent.

After my first year coaching Terry, I called up Phil Jackson, head coach of the world champion Chicago Bulls in the NBA, to pick his brain after reading his book *Sacred Hoops*. He had survived troubles with certain players, and I was looking for some advice regarding similar situations with players of my own. Phil and I spoke about the art of communication with players, particularly the stars who held themselves in high regard but were inconsistent in their mentality toward the team. Phil talked of creating a strategy for dealing with individual players who might be causing distractions.

As the season wore on, Terry became a concern, and I chose to talk to him instead of disciplining him. At times, Terry and I would sit in my office and talk about life, commitment, and teamwork. Some of those conversations went extremely well and others did not. Regardless, Terry became very unpredictable, and the way I was handling the situation may have begun to affect other players. My problem was that I had tried to save him instead of disciplining him, and now when things got difficult, I appeared to be blindly tolerant and not concerned enough about the welfare of the team.

Certain members of the team were certainly watching to see how I would handle this relationship. Terry was a special individual. While he would be the last one to arrive at meetings and the last one on the practice field, he was the first one to talk to a child who was sick or a fan who was wearing his jersey. One day, while in my office discussing a previous incident, Terry said he didn't want to practice and told me that he was going to sit out that day and go home. Sensing that he hadn't had fun on a football field in a while, I asked him if he would drive over early to our practice field with me and just throw the ball around. He obliged, and we simply began to throw the ball back and forth. Then he and I began to run around the field like we were playing in the park, not concerned about the business of the NFL. Before long, we were sweating, laughing, and enjoying the game of football . . . and Terry ended up practicing that afternoon.

I like to think that in moments like that I reached Terry and helped him. But ultimately, I couldn't alter his mentality and our relationship was never what I wanted it to be. Nonetheless I was grateful for those moments, as he was one of my favorite players in New England.

Heading into our second-to-last game of that season, we had to win in order to gain a wild-card play-off berth. Drew Bledsoe was hurt, and Scott Zolak was going to quarterback our team against the formidable 49ers—the team whose image I'd been hired to replicate. It was an incredible challenge but one that our squad embraced. They threw themselves into the competition. The game was incredible, as Scott threw the ball better than he had in years and defensive back Willie Clay intercepted a Steve Young pass, intended for Jerry Rice, late in the game to preserve a 24–21 win. This was a huge moment for us, as we clinched a play-off berth and did it without Drew and three of our top players. I knew firsthand that my former players and fellow coaches hated to lose but I like to think that at least a few of my close friends within the 49ers' organization were somewhat proud of our success that afternoon. In any case, the Niners lost that game with the same style and class that they showed during their previous winning seasons.

I wish I could say the same about how we handled our own defeat the following week. The next week would be our final regular-season game, and the outcome would have no effect on our team's standings in the play-offs. We were playing legendary coach Bill Parcells and the New York Jets. They beat us 31–10, and while it hurt, as all losses do, I was ready to get our team prepared for a play-off run. That is, until the postgame player interviews. One of our top defenders told reporters that we had been "outcoached." The Boston media ran with it, and within a day it leaked out that the ownership was going to review my status at season's end.

We returned to Boston to prepare for the play-off game against the Jacksonville Jaguars. The story around town was focused not on our game but on my job status. It was a terrible distraction for the entire team. I can remember stating that the front office needed to make some sort of comment to quiet the rumors that were growing each day, but the Kraft family was on vacation out of the country and couldn't be reached. Finally, on Friday, Robert Kraft made a statement saying my job was secure, but it was too late—the media already had their story, and we had a mounting distraction.

During the game we had a chance to take the lead in the fourth quarter, but we dropped a short touchdown pass and had to settle for a field goal. On the very next possession, the Jaguars' QB, Mark Brunell, threw a bomb to Jimmy Smith to put the game out of reach. Our season ended, and the frenzy calling for my job in Boston began.

Regardless of what the front office intended, during my third year in New England there was a sense that the writing was on the wall. The lead stories seemed to focus on my job status instead of on the team. Despite all the uncertainty during the off-season, we got off to a great start. We were leading our division at the midway point of the schedule and had arrived at our bye week with a 6-2 record after beating the Arizona Cardinals. Our team was flying high, led by great performances by Drew, and ready to attack the second half of the season, but for whatever reason, our momentum turned south. We never recovered, and I couldn't find a way to get us back on track.

We went on to lose five of the next six games. The media and fans were not happy with our performance and were not afraid to let us know. As the head coach, I was prepared to take the heat. I was okay with that because it is part of the profession, but it wore on us all.

One night late that season, I was tossing and turning and finally realized that a good night's sleep was not an option. I flipped on the television and started rolling through the channels until I stopped on the movie *The Babe*, in which John Goodman played Babe Ruth. I recognized Babe in a Boston Braves uniform at the plate. He had recently been traded from the Yankees to the Braves. He had started the season playing well, but was finishing it playing injured. He was not delivering, and he was hearing it from the nearby fans hanging over the railing. He remained poised and once even smiled at the fans. As he went through his at bat, the count got to 0-2 and the fans got even worse. The Babe just smiled, soaking it all in. On the next pitch he connected, and the ball sailed over the right center-field wall for a home run.

As he rounded third base, trotting toward home plate, the fans turned and began to cheer for him, accepting him. Then it hit me. *The New England fans just want to win!* In essence, the fans at Foxboro were the same as the ones at Braves Field. Generations had been taught to love their local sports teams and hate anyone or anything that got in the way. That night, I realized that the same fans yelling at Babe Ruth were yelling at me—they just wanted to win!

I woke up the next morning with a deeper understanding of and appreciation for the New England fans. What I realized was that we all wanted exactly the same thing: to win. Once I comprehended that, I knew that the only chance I had of making that happen was to go about doing things the best way I could. I needed to compete every day. I was going to control what I could and enjoy each moment of coaching football. I was going to coach my tail off the next day, week, or month and not be concerned about my future. The owner would make his decision eventually, but in the meantime I was going to have a blast coaching ball.

Entering our final game of that season against the Baltimore Ravens, I decided to change things up. On Saturday morning prior to the game, we had our walk-through at Foxboro Stadium, and instead of going into our team meeting room, where I would typically address the players, I took our guys into the visiting team's locker room to give them a different setting for what promised to be a very different Saturday-morning meeting. Until this point, I had been careful to keep our routines the same and stay the course, which were the only factors I could really control. However, I wanted to get my team's attention in a special way, to let them know we were going to compete to the very end of our season.

When I started my speech, I wasn't sure exactly where it was headed, but in my heart I knew it was likely one of the last times I would be addressing the team at the stadium. I wanted not only to inspire them but also to leave them with something they could take with them long after our days together ended. As soon as I began, I knew that what I was going to talk about went way beyond the next day's game against the Ravens. I talked from the inner depths of my being, the same place that I had stored much of the emotion of the past three years. I made it clear that despite the storm that circled our organization and, more specifically, my coaching tenure in New England, they could and should play freely tomorrow and worry about nothing else. I let them know that there was nothing anybody could say or do to me at that point that would distract me from giving them my all tomorrow, and I asked, just one more time, that they do the same. As I look back on it now, that was truly a "win one for the Gipper" speech in true Knute Rockne fashion. I wanted to finish that season 8-8 and avoid going out with a losing record, no matter what it took. So, one last time, we were going to compete to the bitter end.

During my three years with the Patriots, there had been plenty of decisions that could have been made differently, as with any NFL organization and coaching staff. But that didn't really matter to the fifty-three men in that locker room. I just wanted them to play well one more time and to compete freely with no distractions.

The next morning I met with Robert Kraft and pressed him to give me a straight answer about my fate. If this was to be my final game as a Patriot, I told him, I wanted to enjoy it.

He told me that I would be fired after the regular season.

Ironically, on that gray, wintry New England afternoon, we went on to defeat the red-hot Baltimore Ravens 20–3. Winning that day with such loyal players and enjoying what would be my final game in New England is still one of my all-time favorite memories on an NFL sideline. Finishing up 8-8 was particularly meaningful to me because we had seized that day.

Leaving the field for the last time, I had no real idea of what was next for me, but I had a feeling that something good was just about to happen.

There I was, with two years remaining on my contract, realizing what an important opportunity I had to reevaluate my career and my life in general. I knew that I didn't want to be an assistant coach and wasn't even sure I wanted to put on another headset. I had a number of thoughts running through my mind about what to do next. The challenges and rewards of coaching had been phenomenal, but at the same time it seemed like there was some disconnect between my way of looking at things and the expectations of the profession. I knew what I loved, and I knew what I didn't, but I just couldn't quite see how it would all fit together.

Unfortunately, I was still learning how to be a head coach while in New England. As with the Jets, I did not know myself well enough to teach my philosophy to the owner, the front office, and the support staff. After all I had been through, I was still searching for the exact vision and philosophy that would ensure my future success.

As hard as it is to admit, I needed those challenges and some adversity to bring forth my truths, soon to be revealed.

I left the NFL knowing that wherever I ended up next, my job would be to coach every part of the organization and be sure that we all had one heartbeat, one voice. I now understand that different cultures could exist in the front and back offices, but to succeed, these elements need to be in sync. A head coach should be able to hire his own coaching staff if he wants a cohesive unit and also have a strong hand in selecting players. Confidence and trust are vital to a successful organization, and leadership must be supported unconditionally—to the bitter end, if necessary.

Ultimately, I learned that success in the NFL depends on all parts of the organization working together to field a championship team. The competition is so intense and the level of expertise so evenly matched that only the strongest survive. The strongest, I firmly believe, are those that are the most unified as an organization.

As I mulled over my next career move and worked my way through a process of self-discovery, I talked to a close network of friends, in both the media and the business world, about the possibilities outside coaching. We explored ideas such as providing around-the-clock NFL coverage, not unlike what the NFL Network does today. I also wrote league-related articles for CNNSI.com and was asked to be a spokesperson for NFL Youth Football.

Although my schedule was active, I began to feel a bit lost, as none of these "side projects" were gaining traction for the next phase of my career. Without a doubt, I had been enjoying the extra time with my family, watching my kids play sports and just being a dad around the house. In particular, having the freedom to travel and watch my oldest son Brennan's senior season playing tight end for the University of Pittsburgh is one of my most cherished memories.

But I began to feel the squeeze. I was coming up on the final year of my contract in the fall of 2000, and I knew that there would soon be a flurry of job openings in both the college ranks and the NFL. Unfortunately, I still did not have a concrete plan about what to do next.

Before I could start looking at my options, however, I had to think back to the advice of my good friend Monte Kiffin: "You've got to have a philosophy." I couldn't help but wonder what would have happened if only I had seriously asked myself about my own philosophy. If I was ever going to get the chance to run an organization again, I would have to be prepared with a philosophy that would drive all my actions.

PART TWO

THE POWER TO
WIN FOREVER

7

PHILOSOPHY AS
THE FOUNDATION

Both in New York and in New England, we had so many things working well, but we still couldn't pull it all together the way it needed to be. I was fairly sure I knew what I had right, but what I needed to get was a clear view of what was missing.

It was during this post–New England period of contemplation and reflection that I found myself rereading the works of Coach John Wooden. I had been digging deep into past influences of all kinds, but this was the one that made it all click for me.

Coach Wooden's career was legendary, and I had read his books before, but something about the experiences I'd had with the Jets, the 49ers, and most recently the Patriots led me to see things in a new way. What especially jumped out at me was how long it took him to really find his groove. After that first title, in his sixteenth season as UCLA head basketball coach, Coach Wooden went on to win ten out of the next twelve national championships before retiring. He fell just one very close game short of winning nine in a row. For some reason, I had never realized it had taken sixteen years to get his UCLA team to that level.

Coach Wooden's real breakthrough came the moment he had developed his philosophy in a full, complete, and systematic way. Like Marv Levy, who led the Bills to win all those division championships I had seen hanging in the stadium years earlier, Coach Wooden had figured out how to not just win a game or have one great season but *Win Forever.*

The wealth of detail that went into that knowledge was incredible. He had figured out absolutely everything about his program—his belief system, his philosophy, his delivery, and a million other details that made that first championship possible. He had figured it out so completely that he could re-create it year after year after year. Even more important, he had done more than just become aware of all those details inside his own mind. He had refined them to the point that he could explain them to the people around him. I think a great part of his genius was that he was able to explain his beliefs and tie them back into a clear vision that brought it all together into a single team effort.

This exciting eureka moment of insight I got while reading Coach Wooden's book was immediately followed by the less thrilling reminder that with two head coaching failures already on my résumé, not only was I unlikely to get sixteen years to figure all that out for myself—I'd be lucky to get sixteen *months.*

It was time to get moving.

My life in the next weeks and months was filled with writing notes and filling binders. For years, I had ideas about coaching, always challenging the position groups, defensive squads, and teams that I coached to do things in an extraordinary way. But while I had a sense inside me of what we needed, I hadn't articulated it very well. I didn't have the details worked out in my own mind so that I could lay them out clearly and convincingly to anybody else. So,

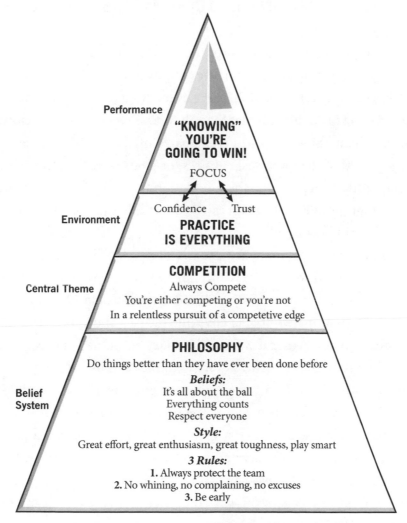

Win Forever
Working to Maximize Your Potential

Performance

**"KNOWING"
YOU'RE
GOING TO WIN!**

FOCUS

Confidence   Trust

Environment

**PRACTICE
IS EVERYTHING**

COMPETITION

Central Theme

Always Compete
You're either competing or you're not
In a relentless pursuit of a competetive edge

PHILOSOPHY
Do things better than they have ever been done before

Beliefs:
It's all about the ball
Everything counts
Respect everyone

Belief
System

Style:
Great effort, great enthusiasm, great toughness, play smart

3 Rules:
1. Always protect the team
2. No whining, no complaining, no excuses
3. Be early

IF YOU WANT TO WIN FOREVER, ALWAYS COMPETE

in the fall of 2000, I forced myself to go through the process of nailing it down, and it was the discipline of working at it that made it happen. By December I finally had a clear, organized template of my core values, my philosophy, and—most important—my overarching vision for what I wanted to stand for as a person, a coach, and a competitor.

If I ever coached again, I promised myself, I was going to build an organization that could win forever. I would build it on the foundation of a single, basic vision where everything we did was centered on wanting to do things better than they have ever been done before. Rather than thinking of different parts of the team as different groups with different styles, cultures, or goals, I wanted this basic competitive thought to be the foundation for everything, from the most high-profile performances to the details that no one but us would ever know about.

I knew that in order for any program I developed to achieve this, it would have to come from within me. It would have to be built on my experience, my core instincts, and my beliefs. So I had to start by looking within myself. As I dove into my past and looked around, I realized that whether it was on the court or on the field, as a dad or as a husband, I was always trying to please those around me. I always wanted to do really well at whatever I was doing. Then it hit me. I had always *competed* to be the best I could be: a great son to my parents, a great brother, a great friend, a great player, a great team member, and now a great husband and father. When I asked myself when I was happiest and most fulfilled and what I stood for, the concept of competition was connected to every one of my responses. Then, in a flash, it hit me: *I am a competitor!*

That simple realization had an incredible impact on everything that was to follow. It was a great personal truth for me, and from that point forward, everything started to fall in line. It became a way to define myself and it was clear that I needed to make competition the central theme in my approach.

At the base of the Win Forever pyramid, the foundation is the philosophy. I collected all of the things that I believed were important in my life and in football and from that I derived the philosophy for Win Forever. What Win Forever means to me is aspiring to be the best you can be, or as I like to refer to it, "maximizing your potential." But Winning Forever is not about the final score; it's about competing and striving to be the best. If you are in this pursuit, then you're already winning.

Also at this foundational level, my philosophy has this vision: Do things better than they have ever been done before. This level consists of a variety of philosophical beliefs for any organization I would build. These covered the elements of the game, human performance, and organizational structure that were most important to me. They included what would be the most important phrase in my next football program, "It's All About the Ball," and the directives known as the Three Rules:

Rule 1. Always Protect the Team
Rule 2. No Whining, No Complaining, No Excuses
Rule 3. Be Early

I also added behavioral, or style, elements: We would perform with great energy, great enthusiasm, and great toughness, and play smart, all while respecting everything and everyone involved in the process.

On the next level of the Win Forever pyramid I put what I'd come to realize was the central theme of my life as a coach: competition. As I had learned through the process of self-discovery, competition is at my personal core, so it would be foolish not to put it at the core of any program I ran. And if I were ever to find myself in an organization where competition didn't play a central role, then I should immediately recognize that I was in the wrong place. I knew that any program that didn't embrace competition had better look for another coach. Other coaches might be successful with an entirely different theme at the center of their programs, but I knew I could only be successful if I focused on what was true to me. My programs would be built on the concept "Always Compete." In line with this, every member of my program would have no choice but to perform in a relentless pursuit of a competitive edge. That concept would carry over to our practice field, where we would compete to find new ways to raise the level of competition in practice each day. Whether it was through entertainment, practical jokes, or straight-up competition, the program I would lead would always be in a relentless pursuit of a competitive edge.

The third level of the pyramid is about the importance of practice. After decades of coaching football at different levels, I was prepared to boldly state that "Practice Is Everything." By placing practice on a high level of the pyramid, I was making a statement. We would never accept having a poor practice or taking a day off. There would be no choices. For us to do things better than they have ever been done before, I believed that we had to practice at the highest level, the most competitive level. I promised myself that I was going to be absolutely relentless in pursuing any competitive edge I could. With consistently competitive practices, players would ultimately reach a point where they could perform in the absence of fear, due to the confidence they had gained by practicing so well. Ideally, they would then learn to trust the process, themselves, and their teammates. When a performer has supreme confidence in himself and can trust all the people around him and the schemes they are running, he is finally free to totally focus and become immersed in his performance. This is where great performers and great teams acquire a most cherished characteristic . . . they *know* they are going to win. When you know you're going to win, you don't doubt or worry. You can actually perform with a "quieted mind," in the absence of fear. It is my job to orchestrate this "knowing" throughout the entire process in every aspect of my next program—a responsibility I would welcome.

8

ALWAYS COMPETE

Lots of people talk about competition, especially those who seek to achieve high performance no matter what the profession. In my experience, however, the real essence of competing is often misunderstood. Competition to me is not about beating your opponent. It is about doing your best; it is about striving to reach your potential; and it is about being in relentless pursuit of a competitive edge in everything you do.

As I worked through that process of developing my vision and plan for success, I decided that competition had to be at the heart of everything we would do—absolutely everything. Our stated goal would be to "do things better than they have ever been done before." When you think about it, that is a statement about competition in its purest form. However successful you may be, there is always some element you can improve upon, some achievement to exceed.

I can't say this any more loudly or any more clearly: *Competition is the central theme* in the Win Forever philosophy. It is absolutely essential to our program. If food, water, and sleep are essential in Maslow's hierarchy of needs, competition is at the core of Win Forever's philosophical needs. Where Nike says, "Just Do It," we say, "If you want to Win Forever, Always Compete." Competition would become everything to the players and coaches in my next program.

Competition is typically defined as a contest between individuals, groups, teams, or nations; it is a test of skills. In my world, however, competition is much more than that. It is a mentality, an outlook, and a way of approaching every day. The traditional definition of competition requires having an opponent. For players, the real "opposition" is not necessarily the team they are matched up against in a given week—far from it. The real opposition is the challenge to remain focused on maximizing their abilities in preparation for the game.

I have worked for plenty of teams where coaches spend the week or even the month leading up to a "big" game talking down the opposition. They fuel traditional rivalries and do whatever they can to build up the other team as the enemy. Of course, this approach wins games for many teams, but I don't agree. The essence of my message about competing has nothing to do with the opponent. My competitive approach is that "it's all about us." If we've really done the preparation to elevate ourselves to our full potential, it shouldn't matter whom we're playing.

Once I understood that we were competing with ourselves, it changed my view of future opponents. Many people confuse "opponent" with "enemy," but in my experience, that is extremely unproductive. My opponents are not my enemies. My opponents are the people who offer me the opportunity to succeed. The tougher my opponents, the more they present me with an opportunity to live up to my full potential and play my best. From an extreme perspective, that's a reason to love them, not to hate them. At the end of the day, that opponent is the person who makes you into the best competitor you can be.

Thus, a Win Forever team or organization holds opponents in high regard because they are the ones who call on us to reach our potential. In our practices, we always end each day with our best offensive players competing against our best defensive players to create the most competitive situations. It is crucial to maximizing the development of the team.

Of course, when we say that the competition is "all about us," that doesn't mean that we don't think about our opponents. Of course we do. We think about them a lot. But what we do is try to understand their makeup and nature. We want to center our focus on what we can control, which is us. We have no control over what our opponents do; we can only control what we do. We want to maximize our potential, and to do that we must focus our energy and efforts on ourselves.

These thoughts about being a competitor are not necessarily all insights that I came up with on my own. Some are simply truths about performance that I have observed by being around extraordinary achievers during my career. I have had the good fortune of working with or admiring from afar many individuals who have taught me about competing. Among all of those people, the greatest individual competitor I have come in close contact with is Hall of Fame wide receiver Jerry Rice. I worked with him in San Francisco, and I have always said that the 49ers had many great competitors in the organization, but Jerry stood above the rest.

From my very first days on the staff, it was obvious to me that Jerry felt he had to prove to himself and his teammates that he was great. And this was not just on game day; it was during walk-throughs, training camp, off-season workouts, and even charity events. The beauty of it was that his mentality became a part of the 49ers culture, and Ronnie Lott, Steve Young, and others followed suit. Still, Jerry was different from anyone else.

As I got to know Jerry, I learned that he had to prove who he was every single chance he got. Apparently he had this drive at an early age, and it was an approach he carried over to his NFL career. Whatever it was, Jerry would give everything he had to beat you. He came to practice taped up, in full pads, and ready to go every day, and he'd finish in the end zone every time he caught the ball. He is easily recognized as one of the great competitors of all time. When I say Jerry competed at everything, I mean it. I saw it for myself.

During my first year in San Fransico, there was a celebrity basketball game at Santa Clara University pitting the 49ers from the 1980s against the 49ers of the 1990s. As a new coach on the staff and interested in 49ers history, I went to watch the game. The score was fairly even, and I was watching some of the guys and their personalities. Jerry played really well, scoring a bunch of points, then checking out of the game for a while. He was having fun on the bench signing autographs and talking to fans.

Then, over the loudspeaker, the announcer said that Carlton Williamson had become the leading scorer in the game. I looked around and Jerry was already on a knee checking back into the game. He went in for several minutes, scored twelve points in a wild flurry, and then took himself back out again. It was all just to make sure he was the leading scorer in the game.

He didn't say anything to anybody, but it was so clear what he was all about. He may not even remember doing that, yet it was a magnificent illustration that to him everything was a personal competition. Basketball, of course, had nothing to do with it.

As a great competitor, Jerry understood that by staying in the mind-set of always competing he could develop the awareness to capture the "opportunities within opportunities" that other people might miss. In other words, he was constantly seeking a competitive edge. It helps to always be searching for that tiny edge in whatever you're doing—even if it's small, silly stuff—because that's how you are going to catch things that someone else might not when it really matters. It's an extremely powerful tool.

Just as important as that competitive intensity was the fact that you could see without a doubt that Jerry was really competing with himself. He never allowed his success or failure to be defined by anyone else. Jerry Rice's ability to maintain his competitive focus made him into one of the great figures in the history of sports. I think his example is an unusually valuable one.

Adopting an all-out "always compete" approach to your passions does not necessarily come without a price. For example, it may be difficult to get a good night's sleep if your mind is occupied by thoughts of doing things better than they have ever been done before, or being the best you can be. In extreme cases, you may be faced with a decision to uproot yourself and your family in order to pursue a professional opportunity.

One of the first, but not the last, times that brought this into focus came when I left UOP, after coaching for three years as a graduate assistant. Something needed to change, and my two choices were to coach at Moreau Catholic High School in the Bay Area, which would have been convenient, or to pack up a U-Haul and move to Fayetteville, Arkansas, to coach under Monte Kiffin and Lou Holtz, who had just been named head coach at the University of Arkansas. At the time, it was just Glena and I, but nonetheless I made the difficult choice to shift our entire lives just so I could pursue that competitive opportunity.

I want to be honest about what it takes to compete at an extreme level—but I don't for a minute want to scare anyone away from embracing competition. Having the drive to always compete doesn't necessarily mean you have to either make the choices I've made or not compete at all. That couldn't be further from the truth. You can compete to be a good student, compete to be a good friend, compete to be a good dad, or a husband or wife. My point is to make conscious choices about what you compete at, and always compete to do your best at whatever that is. The idea is that you can be a great competitor at whatever you're doing. You can direct this competitive mentality to serve you in all aspects of your life.

9

PRACTICE IS EVERYTHING

The uncompromising core belief of Win Forever is to "do things better than they have ever been done before." This includes football practice. It might seem obvious that, as a coach, I would say that good practice sessions are important. But my view of practice is different from most others'. To me, practice is not just something that is necessary for a team to prepare itself for game day. Rather, practice is one of the many places where we compete to be the best.

It is my belief that how we practice makes just as important a statement about who we are as how we play the games. How we practice defines who we are. It is not only something we have to do in order to compete, but our practice is a competitive activity in and of itself. Practice is something we want to be the best at for its own sake. As I began to develop my thoughts about this and to write them down, I recalled a great example to illustrate this point.

During the year following my last season with the Patriots, I had been asked by the league offices to critique a youth program the NFL was conducting. I observed two different practices in an afternoon, one in Brooklyn and one in the Bronx. The first practice was well organized and disciplined, and the drills had been set up properly for a youth team. I expected to see more or less the same thing at my next stop. When we got to the Bronx, however, I didn't have to see a thing to realize that my assumption had been completely mistaken.

We had parked out of view of the field where the second practice was taking place, but from the moment I got out of the car, I could hear it: whistles, kids, and coaches, all sounding somewhat unlike the practice I'd come from. Here there was something very different—it was the energy. As I hurried around the corner and saw the levels of activity and emotion unfolding, I was able to see the energy and enthusiasm that I live for as a coach. Despite the fact that both teams clearly had the same gear, the same facilities, and players of comparable ability, this practice and the one I had just come from were two utterly different experiences. From the moment I got out of the car, I sensed this was going to be a better practice.

As I got closer, I could hear coaches speaking in Spanish and English, but the language didn't matter. The players could interpret the passion, energy, and excitement. It was so clear to me that these coaches were the source of the difference, and it just blew me away. You could have put any group on the field with that staff and the results would have been the same. Obvious passion and competitive desire to play football dominated the scene.

I know that if I were a kid on that field, I would have loved this practice, as it reminded me of my first experiences in Pop Warner. In the first year I signed up to play football, I was ten years old and excited to get started in the local Pop Warner league. I don't know if they still do it, but in those days when you signed up, they sent you a workout routine to get in shape for training camp. For the most part, I think it was something to give kids a sense of what football camp was going to be like; it wasn't something that any of the kids I knew actually did. But at ten years old I took off and started running hills in my hometown to get in shape. No one told me that we were even going to be tested—I was just crazy about the idea that when the time came to be tested, I was going to be as ready as I possibly could. I never even thought twice about it. I knew that if I wanted to do really well when practice came, I had better start running. Because I understood the link between practicing and my goal of being ready to play, it quickly became something that I wanted to do for myself.

There I was, an NFL coach with many years of experience, and it was a youth program that made me realize how crucial the energy of the coaches was to create a great practice atmosphere. It was so obvious that coaches were the factor that dictated and controlled the energy of practice. It was there in the Bronx that I realized that coaches are ultimately responsible for maintaining a high level of intensity for every practice session. Once I realized it was our responsibility to establish the tone and energy of practice, I had a newfound vision about how important it would be to motivate my next staff on a daily basis. I learned that if you want to have great practice sessions, you have to prepare your staff to have great days. That was exactly what I witnessed on the practice field that day in the Bronx. The passion and the excitement that coaches bring to the field will transfer directly to the players and will allow you to create a competitive practice environment, not to mention a fun one. I declared forevermore that in my coaching career, we would practice with more energy and more excitement than anyone else in football.

PART THREE

WIN FOREVER
AT USC

10

GETTING THE JOB AT USC

By December 2000, I had gone through an enormous process of self-discovery and created a vision and philosophy. I was excited and ready to present my approach to any athletic director or owner who would listen. More important, I was as confident in myself as I had ever been.

My next team would be built around the goal of maximizing everyone's potential. We would strive to "do things better than they have ever been done before" with competition as our central theme. With my thoughts down on paper in a new way, I felt more ready, more prepared, and more focused than I had ever been before. When my next coaching opportunity came along, I knew exactly how I intended to approach every aspect of building a new program. All that remained was to find a job where I could put it all to the test.

There were only a few job opportunities that year that truly interested me. One morning, my longtime friend and lawyer, Gary Uberstine, called. "Pete, the University of North Carolina has an opening. Do you want to go for it?"

I was fired up, so my response was an overwhelming yes, as UNC had a long-standing athletic tradition and was in a great location. After showing a strong interest in the job, we were told that their athletic department was not interested in offering an interview. Their reason was my lack of recent college coaching experience.

Not to be discouraged, we forged ahead and hoped another attractive opportunity would come along. We waited and stayed positive, resolved to stick to the plan we had set. Finally, the phone rang. This time it was a school near the ocean but on the opposite coast. The next thing I knew, I was on my way to meet with the athletic director at USC.

It was easy to recognize him when I arrived—after all, I'd grown up with a poster of him on my wall. Mike Garrett was USC's first Heisman Trophy winner in 1965 and went on to have a fantastic professional career with the Kansas City Chiefs and the San Diego Chargers. He was someone I had always held in very high regard. Mike was an explosive and hard-nosed back, the first in a long line of legendary running backs whose performances resulted in the University of Southern California being dubbed "Tailback U."

After his NFL career, Mike quickly made his mark outside football and earned a law degree. He returned to USC to become its athletic director in 1993. When his office called requesting the interview, I knew that the very proud and storied football program was off course and that the pressure was on Mike to find the right coach to get it back on track.

Before I traveled to California, I studied the other candidates who were being interviewed to figure out what I was up against. I thought back to some advice given to me years earlier by the legendary Jim Valvano, who was the head basketball coach at North Carolina State when I was the defensive coordinator there. Then, I had been in the process of preparing to interview for the head coaching job at UOP. Coach Valvano called me to his office one Sunday morning to talk about the interviewing process and work on my strategy. As we sat there for over four hours, he taught me a number of interviewing tactics that I will never forget.

Coach Valvano told me that my goal should be to walk out of the interview with "no negatives." Every comment, phrase, or story must be positive, and I had to be prepared to talk only about things that put me in the best light. No matter what the topic, it was my job to turn every answer into a response that highlighted my strong points. Like his point guard, who controlled the court, or my middle linebacker, who controlled our defense, I had to control the interview. He taught me that if they asked a question that I couldn't answer, then I shouldn't answer it but instead find a way to turn the question to something I could talk about comfortably, positively, and honestly. He explained the importance of being disciplined in that setting and avoiding any and all negative thoughts. If I spoke with positivity and confidence, it would be evident that I believed in myself, and that belief was what the interviewer would be looking for. Coach Valvano's advice, like so much else in life, came down to practice: The bottom line was that if I was to control the interview, I would have to be prepared on so many levels that I could speak about a variety of subjects with conviction and strength no matter which way the conversation went.

I did not end up getting the head coaching job at UOP. Bobby Cope, a longtime friend and mentor did, and I joined Bobby as his offensive coordinator. Next time around, the advice from Coach Valvano ran through my head once again as I prepared for my upcoming interview with USC at the Sheraton Hotel near the airport. Not only was I ready to present my new personal and coaching philosophy, but I was also confident knowing that Coach Valvano was there in spirit.

I walked into the Sheraton Hotel and sat down with Mike and then senior associate athletic director Daryl Gross, with whom I had worked at the New York Jets. A large table sat in the middle of the room with two notepads on it. Mike explained their situation and why he believed USC had recently begun to slide. He took me through his game plan for his search for a new coach and made it clear right up front that he was not worried about the media during the process. He was focused on finding the right guy for the job, regardless of how long it took; what we were there to talk about that day was whether or not I might be that person.

As I listened to Mike, I knew with more and more certainty that I was in the right place. I couldn't help but feel a growing eagerness to present what I had been developing over the past few months. I began by explaining what I thought had occurred in New York and New England. As Mike asked me questions, I didn't always respond in a way that answered the question directly, but I responded in a way that conveyed every ounce of my vision and philosophy.

When it came time for me to present my vision and plan, I stated my intentions in the clearest and boldest way that I could think of.

"Mike, our goal is simple: to do things better than they have ever been done before."

As I prepared to elaborate, I could tell that both Mike and Daryl were intrigued. I took them through my philosophical approach, discussing everything from the central theme of competition that would be synonymous with the program, the importance of practice, defensive schemes, recruiting, adjusting to the college game, handling the Los Angeles media, and what I felt it would take to get USC back on track to be the program it had been and deserved to be. With each statement I gave, I felt more confident. The more confident I felt, the more excited I became.

As the interview came to an end, Mike asked me what I would say in my first press conference and our first team meeting. As I began to answer him, I felt as though I already was the head football coach at USC and they just had to formally offer me the job. After Mike, Daryl, and I had shaken hands and I was leaving the Sheraton, I felt great. I knew that I had just delivered a comprehensive explanation of how I would lead their storied program, but more important, I knew that I had just presented who I was as a person and a football coach in a comprehensive and completely authentic way for the first time in my life.

I spent the next few days in the beach area, relaxing by the water and enjoying the LA environment. In fact, I was on the beach when the phone call came in the afternoon of December 15, 2000. It was official—I was the new head coach of one of the most successful and storied programs in the history of college football.

We knew that my selection would be met with a fair amount of criticism. After all, I was an NFL coach with two firings on my résumé, no recent college experience, and unfamiliarity with Pac-10 football. I certainly wasn't the first choice of a lot of fans—and for many I wasn't even on the radar at all. The buzz had surrounded three successful college coaches. None of them seemed to want the job, but I think the general expectation among the fans and boosters was that they were going to get one of the names they knew. When I was announced, it really caught people off guard—and understandably so. The coach who had just been fired at USC was a former NFL coach, and because it all sounded so similar to them, there was a real firestorm. I was definitely coming in with a lot to prove in the eyes of the community.

I knew that my first public appearance at the USC press conference would be crucial in setting the stage for future success. I had learned many lessons during my years facing very tough media markets in both New York and New England, and I was ready for anything.

Because I was personally so clear about the direction of USC football and really feeling confident in the style and philosophy I intended to bring to the program, I actually couldn't wait for the press conference to begin, even though I knew the stakes were incredibly high. I just laid out my philosophy for the program for all the world to hear. I told the assembled press, "Talk is cheap right now—we have to get to work. My teams are going to play hard, they're going to play with enthusiasm, they're going to play with great intensity." When they asked me how long it would take to win, I simply said, "We'll be good when we're good. My goal is to win right now."

I heard later that some of my comments seemed a bit bold and stern, but I was just living the philosophy that I had laid out months earlier for myself and my future teams. I wasn't worried about the transition from the NFL to college because I had been coaching college kids for years—I just got them when they were a few years older. All I could think of was that I was about to embark on the adventure of a lifetime. After an entire career spent learning the game of football, I finally had a comprehensive, authentic philosophy that came straight from my heart and now had the opportunity to put it into motion. The real test of my Win Forever philosophy would be what happened once it was applied.

In my nine years at USC, we worked hard at applying the approach and stuck to the core beliefs that we could and would do things better than they have ever been done before. We competed in everything we did, from practice to teaching to showing up early.

We worked to gain confidence and erase fear by practicing for every contingency. And we stayed constantly focused on maximizing the potential of everyone in the organization. We applied ourselves and our philosophy diligently, and we started to win. I cannot even describe how grateful I felt and how fortunate I was to lead that historic program.

11

LAYING GROUND RULES

After the first press conference, it was time to focus on hiring a staff and recruiting a team. Finding the right coaching staff was important, and fortunately, we were able to put together a great group. In the early meetings, we spent a lot of time laying out what the program was going to look like and how we wanted it to work. I needed the coaches to teach the players, so I needed to teach them first.

I explained that we would have a new way of thinking. I told them the whole story, from Coach Wooden on. After that, I talked about how it would all fit together. I told them where we were going, how we were going to compete, how we were going to practice, and how we were going to build our team and coach the players to be great. This was my philosophy, I explained, and while it would guide the program, I also wanted them to think about their own philosophies. I wanted them to think about how they could utilize that same approach to develop their messages for their position groups as well as to make themselves the best they could possibly be.

It was the start of a tradition built around keeping everyone connected to the philosophy. I would bring the staff together at the beginning of every season to repeat those lessons.

Once we had set the vision, "do things better than they have ever been done before," we had to pursue it. We needed the players to buy in. We needed to make sure they understood how to battle, how to compete, and how to push themselves to the limits both physically and mentally. That process began with our first workout.

In our first workout with our players that spring, we tested them. For two hours our staff put them through the grinder. Sprints, drills, up-downs, agility tests, and more were part of our workout. The only goal was to make it so difficult that the players would never forget that day.

At the end of the afternoon, the players were drenched in sweat and our coaches were satisfied. We had set the tone and begun to ingrain the commitment to working hard. But we were not done with that day's work.

I told the players to meet me at the fifty-yard line in the Los Angeles Memorial Coliseum at 10:30 P.M. and we would finish our workout there. As the players left the Howard Jones Practice Field, I could hear them asking one another, "What are we doing at the Coli?" The funny thing is, I didn't know the answer either, but my instinct told me that we had to be there.

The Los Angeles Memorial Coliseum has hosted the Super Bowl, a World Series, the Olympics in 1932 and 1984, and John F. Kennedy's acceptance speech at the 1960 Democratic National Convention, among many other events. It was also the site of USC home games.

After leaving the practice field, I decided that we needed a rope. After learning that the local fire station was across the street from campus, I walked over to Station #15 and asked if I could borrow their longest and thickest rope. With a "what is this guy up to?" look, they obliged, and over my shoulder went a very heavy rope.

Ten P.M. arrived and I stood on the fifty-yard line awaiting the players. Ten fifteen came, and still I stood alone with just our staff. Finally, around 10:25, I began to hear cleats echoing in the tunnel of the Coliseum as the players began their walk to the field. Soon the tunnel was echoing with their expectant chatter. As they spotted the coaches waiting for them at the fifty-yard line, they went dead silent. Some players were dressed to work out, and others were coming from class with their backpacks, but no one knew what to expect and none were prepared for what happened next.

At the time, I knew only a few players by name, so I called out to Carson Palmer and Troy Polamalu: "Carson, Troy—give me your best eleven on offense and your best eleven on defense. We're having a tug of war."

Guys started ripping their shirts off, tying up their shoes—they were ready to compete, and the energy of the group exploded. Carson and Troy had chosen their squads, and they proceeded to take hold of the rope. "One, two, three!" and the battle was on. The offense took a quick lead, but the defense pulled even. Back and forth they went, with extra players from the defense eventually jumping in to help them try to claim victory. The players were howling and cheering support for one another. Neither side could dominate, and the whole team fell together into a heap of bodies. I called everyone together and asked Carson one question: "Carson, what did we just learn?"

After a long pause by our starting quarterback, I said to myself, *Oh boy, we're in trouble.* He responded, "I dunno, Coach."

I realized he needed some help, so I said, "Carson—didn't we learn that if we're pulling in opposite directions we all can't win as one?"

"Yeah, that's right, Coach!" he quickly responded. My next thought was, *Well, at least he's coachable.*

Then I told them to huddle on the fifty-yard line, everybody back to back, looking out, and with everyone touching. I wanted us leaning on one another totally connected, so close that nothing could come between us.

Standing in the middle of our team, I told them that if we remained as tight as we were at that moment, it didn't matter who came over the walls of this great coliseum to challenge us. Notre Dame, Washington, UCLA, anyone—if we remained close enough so no one could ever come between us, we would win. I told them their coaches were looking for their commitment to this new program, and that we wanted each player, when he was ready, to declare, "I'm in!"

Imagine a clear, dark night inside the Coliseum, with only a few lights illuminating a space that holds more than ninety thousand screaming fans on game day, however tonight this place belonged to us alone. The setting was out of a movie, and the sensations and emotions were running high. I told them to think about the commitment I was asking for but I didn't want them to jump in just because of the excitement of the moment. I told them that when they were ready, truly ready, to commit to being a Trojan, then I wanted them to stop by my office, send me a message, or leave me a note with two simple words—and to firmly understand the importance behind those words, what they meant, and the competition those two words stood for.

Day by day, player by player, it happened.

I'm in. . . . I'm in. . . . I'm in. . . . As each of those guys stopped by and made that affirmative commitment, I could feel the team taking shape, and I became more and more excited about what we could accomplish in the season ahead.

Every year, as you build your team, there always seems to be a critical moment when things either come together or go south. If a coach is lucky enough to sense this moment, he captures it and puts it into proper perspective for his players, and they become stronger and more connected as a result. We had such a moment at USC in the 2001 season that not only changed that team but affected our teams for years to follow.

We flew into Tucson in that first season with a 2-5 record to play the University of Arizona. We had suffered through last-second defeats at the hands of Oregon and Washington and were struggling to find any kind of positive identity.

When we arrived at the stadium, we carried out our day-before-the-game routine of checking out the locker room, dressing out in warm-up gear, and getting a feel for the stadium and the turf. It was designed to be a light workout to get familiar with the surroundings, relax, and stretch our legs following the plane flight. It was still very hot in the desert that afternoon, and when we got to the stadium, the players seemed a bit listless and uninterested. I was concerned, to say the least. As soon as we arrived at the hotel, I gathered the coaches to address the situation. I told them what I thought of the status of the team and, with all my competitive fire, implored them to come up with the most gut-wrenching, emotional, and passionate speech or presentation they could muster for the final Friday-night meeting in preparation for Saturday's game. We knew we had to pull off a miracle to get this team in the right frame of mind.

This night was a real competitive challenge for me and our staff. We had reached a critical moment for our new program, and the way we responded to this challenge could make or break us in this season. We had to run this meeting better than any meeting had ever been run before. Our coaches took the challenge to heart and came up with some speeches that were so ridiculous that the players were stirred by the craziness of their efforts, if nothing else. At the end of the meeting, I felt like we were back on track.

The following night, late in the game, we were leading, but Arizona had come roaring back to make it close. Like the past two conference games, this one could go either way. It all came down to a critical play late in the fourth quarter. Arizona's quarterback dropped back and threw a pass. Our cornerback, Kris Richard, read it perfectly, stepping in front of the intended receiver, and intercepting the ball with impeccable timing. He raced down the sideline, having only to beat the quarterback himself, and with what he would refer to as the old "shake and bake" move, he rumbled into the end zone for the game-securing touchdown.

It was a great moment for our team and for our program. In the locker room following the game, I told them that we had shown that we were a team that knew how to finish. "From this point on, we don't have to lose anymore!" I told them excitedly. And for years to come, we went into every game knowing we had what it took to win.

When I look back on that night in the desert, I realize we had reached a crossroads that we all are faced with now and then, where an opportunity presents itself for things to change forever. I will always be grateful for that weekend when all seemed lost. It felt like we were ready to crumble, but when we needed it most, we stayed with our basic philosophy and continued to compete to the end. Of course, we didn't win every game from then on, but we won a lot of them, and it began when it looked like we were going to hit rock bottom.

After that first season we started a tradition in spring practice. Every year, on the first day of our monthlong spring practice, we would begin with a team meeting. Predictably, the veteran guys would settle into the same seats they had gotten used to during the previous season. That just seems to be human nature.

This meeting would begin by congratulating the guys on being there and on the job they had done the previous season. We'd remind them that we had last year's highlights on a DVD for them to take home and watch whenever they wanted. Then I'd tell them how fired up I was about spring practice and I would tell them to get up and find a different seat. My message was that there was no room for anybody to be thinking that last year's success guaranteed anything for the upcoming season. If they wanted to compete at an uncommon level and live our philosophy, they needed a brand-new perspective on the upcoming season; by changing their seats, at least symbolically, they now found themselves with a new perspective. They could take that DVD and put it in their back pocket. By finding a new seat, they would recommit to capturing the work ethic that would allow them to maximize their potential.

This little ritual may have been a small thing, but it sent a powerful message on a number of levels. Yes, we may have been champions, but it had to be understood that as a program we were never about winning one championship or one Rose Bowl—we were about *owning* the Rose Bowl. That's why, in spite of my pride in our accomplishments as an organization, I never wanted to get too excited about wearing our championship rings or make a big deal about our past success. Why? Because we can't do anything about what has already happened. All we ever really have is the very next moment we are facing. Of course, we always can celebrate, learn, and grow from past experiences, but the very next step we are about to take may be the most important one and we don't want to miss it.

So at the beginning of each spring practice, we'd change seats to look at our world with new eyes. We were making the statement that it was a new year and we were making a fresh start. It's a competitive thought. If we are truly competing, we can never afford to look at things from an old perspective. In essence, we opened each year by celebrating a new beginning from an appropriate and new vantage point.

The football program that we pulled together at USC was composed of millions of details, but we structured those details by always keeping the big picture in view. We wanted to maximize our potential and do everything we did better than it had ever been done before. This meant *everything*, not just as football coaches and players but as human beings. We sought to instill a way of looking at not just football but everything in life as a series of opportunities to become the best versions of ourselves—not according to anyone else's definition of success but according to the one we set for ourselves.

If our vision was to "do things better than they have ever been done before," we knew we would have to support that with a structure—not just an intellectual or conceptual structure but a consistent and clearly expressed set of expectations. These expectations had to be specific and concise enough to be enforceable, but they also needed to be broad enough to work as a flexible teaching tool in a wide variety of situations.

At USC I introduced "Three Rules," which became foundational elements for our program. They may not have translated exactly into all situations but they offered a basic framework that would apply to almost any organization seeking to establish a culture that gets the most out of its people. Here is how we laid it out:

Rule 1. Always Protect the Team
Rule 2. No Whining, No Complaining, No Excuses
Rule 3. Be Early

Protecting the team was all about our players' consciences. We wanted them to be fully aware of what they were doing at all times and to understand that for every decision they made there would be a result that affected the team and ultimately everyone who depended on our success. We wanted them to seek outcomes that would protect their family, their teammates, and their university. It's a great rule, I think, because it's both open-ended and uncompromising.

We utilized Rule #1 in many ways in our program, but collectively we probably leaned on it most of all when dealing with our losses. Fortunately, we didn't have a lot of them, but each one was monumental for us. At times the public perception after a loss was that our program was way off course. In fact we were a lot more resilient than that, and part of that resiliency came from our ability to lean on Rule #1 as a core element of the program. Whether it was Oregon State in 2006, Oregon or Stanford in 2007, or Washington in 2009, when tough losses occurred, we were sure to examine every snap of the game. Whether it was a missed blocking assignment, a personal foul, or a blown read on defense, it was vital that our players understood the importance of every decision they made on every snap. It is easy for a young athlete to lose focus or fail to comprehend the importance of his assignment on each play, but it was our job as a staff to tap into each player's conscience. Rule #1 allowed us to do that. When a play didn't turn out well, we were careful not to frame the analysis in terms of laying blame but rather to point out that when someone failed to execute, it may have been because he did not fully understand his responsibility. As coaches, we wanted to make the impression that everything counted and sometimes experiencing a loss created the best opportunity for that.

Rule #1 was instrumental in protecting our program off the field as well. We were fortunate not to have too many disciplinary issues at USC, and Rule #1 was a major reason why. Our staff understood that we were operating in a college setting bordering Hollywood, where the social scene never lacks excitement, but we needed our players to look out for one another at all times. Understanding what it means to "Always Protect the Team" was enormously beneficial to our program. The upperclassmen became the beacons for Rule #1, taking the younger players under their wing while championing our staff's message.

Rule #2 was almost as simple: "No Whining, No Complaining, No Excuses." Where Rule #1 was about recognizing the consequences of our actions, this one was about our language, or what we refer to as self-talk—and how important it was to take responsibility for yourself and make no excuses. I strongly believe in the power of intentions and wanted everyone in our program to speak in the affirmative. Whereas a negative mentality attracts negative thoughts, a positive approach creates the power of possibilities. (By the way, this rule was borrowed from Coach Wooden's book —thanks, Coach!)

This is not to say that I wanted to sweep problems under the rug or deny that they existed. Far from it. If a player had a direct problem with me or how I was coaching, I not only wanted to hear about it, I felt I needed to. However, there are appropriate times to express these frustrations and that meant my door was always open. If a player was unhappy about his playing time, I wanted him to talk to his coaches before he complained to his teammates. As coaches, we would prefer to deal with issues head-on instead of burying them and would discourage members of our program from complaining or making excuses. By encouraging our players to communicate in such ways, we developed a positive mentality for the entire team.

Rule #2 got its first major test at USC in 2001. It was my first spring as head coach, and our starting QB, Carson Palmer, was having as good a month throwing the football as I had ever seen. An exceptional athlete, Carson stood six feet five inches, weighed 235 pounds, and ran, at that time, a 4.6-second forty-yard dash. In the first fourteen spring practices he had played extremely well and had yet to throw an interception. He was becoming a team leader and his confidence was growing with each workout.

During the final workout which was our annual spring game, Carson tossed his first two interceptions of the spring, and as we stood at the team barbecue afterward, they were obviously affecting him. I asked him what he thought about his performance, and his response was the last thing I expected:

"It's just so typical. I always play well and then screw it up when it matters most."

At that moment I stopped him in his tracks, made him put his tray down, and firmly told him one simple thing. "Carson, you never, *ever*, get to talk that way again."

It was a great example of the power of Carson's negative self-talk. Rather than accepting the challenge to compete to get the best of his self-doubt, he had given in to a negative expectation and expressed it as fact.

Self-talk can be powerful and ultimately can create anticipated outcomes. In Carson's case, it helped to create a negative outcome. But it can also be used to create positive outcomes, and I was determined to help Carson alter his language.

Throughout the summer and fall, when Carson and I spoke, positive affirmations and self-talk were central themes. It wasn't a case of hiding from or sugarcoating the truth. The fact was that Carson was a fabulous football player. I knew it and everyone around him knew it. He just needed to know it too. Two years later, he led our team to a 10-2 record and an Orange Bowl title and captured the Heisman Trophy. He left USC as the Pac-10 all-time leader in passing yards, completions, and total offense. He was also the number one overall pick in the 2003 NFL draft, selected by the Cincinnati Bengals. Those accolades only confirmed the extraordinary level of expectations he deserved to own. As soon as he stopped doubting himself and began to envision positive outcomes, his natural gifts propelled him to great success.

In the 2003–2004 season, our ability to utilize Rule #2 was put to the test. We finished the season 11-1, ranked number one in the Associated Press and *USA Today*/ESPN coaches' poll, but ranked lower in the all important computer poll. The result was that we were left out of the BCS national championship game.

After beating Oregon State to end the season, I can remember sitting at home wondering how the bowl game scenario would shape up. When the polls were released the next morning, my youngest son, Nate, and I were on the computer going through each possibility. We could see the writing on the wall and anticipated that we would likely be left out of the title game.

Driving in to campus that day, I had to prepare a message to deliver to our players during the team meeting that afternoon. I called senior associate athletic director Daryl Gross to discuss the situation, and he told me history proved that whoever was number one in the Associated Press poll usually remained number one, if they won their bowl game. Thus, the message would be simple. If we could beat Michigan in the Rose Bowl, we could still be national champions.

It ended up being a great example of how we use Rule #2, as our players easily could have walked out of that meeting addressing the media with complaints or excuses about the computer poll and the BCS title matchup, but they never wavered. Each member of the team spoke with the same positive voice regarding our bowl game. We were fortunate to represent the Pac-10 in the Rose Bowl, and if we won, we would be crowned national champions. We focused on what we could control and didn't look back as we defeated the Wolverines 28–14, with Matt Leinart tossing three touchdowns and catching another.

Let me be the first to say that following Rule #2 can be difficult. It's often much easier to whine, complain, and make excuses. Trust me, I've been tempted to go down that road many times. It was hard seeing my name on the front pages of the *New York Post* and *Boston Globe* as writers were calling for my job. It was difficult to hear from two different owners that they didn't feel I had what it took to lead their franchises. It was awful to get fired on five separate occasions and move my family around the country. I disliked every minute of it but I found a way not to sanction those opinions and decisions. I held on to the competitive thought that I just needed another chance.

The third and final rule in our program, "Be Early," was all about being organized and showing respect. At USC, we wanted our players in meetings before they started, and more important, we wanted them there with their playbooks open and minds ready to learn. To be early, you must have your priorities in order. You have to be organized to the point where you have a plan and can execute it effectively. Part of teaching players to execute on the field is teaching them to execute off the field as well. We wanted them to understand that by being organized they demonstrated respect for the coaches who called the meeting, for their teammates, and ultimately for themselves. Our players could not choose when to be early and when not to, just as with any other commitment they had made. This made it possible for them to be at their best in our program, by respecting the process and those involved in it.

Rule #3 was also an opportunity for new arrivals to understand the uncommon level of performance we expected from them in every aspect of their lives. This could be an issue with freshmen in particular. Every year there were always one or two young players who wanted to demonstrate their individuality by being the last guy into the meeting, sneaking in right before we started. When we noticed something like that, we would bring the player into our staff room and place him in what we called a roundtable discussion. The player would sit at one end of a long table surrounded by the staff. The coaches would then discuss the importance of being early and being organized. We would tell the player that by being early, he would make every aspect of his life easier. By being organized he would play with more confidence, and by taking notes he would be more prepared. Typically, the player had not realized the rationale behind the rule or how much we thought it said about what we expected from him on and off the field. Once he got the message, not only would he become the first guy in the meetings, but over time he would improve his play and also recognize an important chance to prove his commitment to his teammates.

Limiting ourselves to three rules was a very conscious choice. The scope they cover is broad and is enough to encompass any issue or indiscretion that might arise. It started with a player's conscience, dealt with his language and self-talk, and ended with the discipline and respect it took to do things right. Just like any other organization, a team needs rules and guidelines.

12

COACH YOUR COACHES

The Win Forever philosophy is not just about maximizing the potential of our players. It is about maximizing the potential of everyone in a program or organization. All the principles we use with our players apply to our coaches and other staff members as well. Right down to the core of our being, we believe that our success depends on ensuring that everyone is completely engaged, committed, and in a relentless pursuit of a competitive edge. A big part of my job is creating an environment where this will happen.

As head coach, I set the vision and the philosophy, but it is the coordinators and other coaches who are charged with implementing it on the ground with the players every day. They have to be comfortable with the plan, confident in themselves, and armed with a competitive spirit to do their jobs better than they have ever been done before. We work to ensure this by empowering our coaches and putting them in positions where they are given the opportunity to succeed. I put great emphasis on making sure that I coach our coaches and that our success also helps them develop their own vision and teaching styles.

Just as with our players, I do everything I can to elicit my coaches' competitive drive and strengthen their sense of themselves in their work. I even use many of the same methods that I use with our players to stir up my coaches' competitive energies. I love to stoke little rivalries between the coaches of various position groups. If I do this effectively, the energy trickles right down to the players. If I start messing with someone in the morning staff meeting, you can count on his guys playing that much harder in practice that afternoon. It is a great illustration of how contagious that competitive drive can be.

Our program has its message and its way of speaking, but our staff has great latitude to deliver that message in the way that makes the most sense for them. It is great for them, and it is great for the organization. I'm constantly making suggestions, but they teach the message in their own ways, in their own voices. Some people think this is an unusual way to run a football program, but I honestly can't imagine any other way of getting the results I'm looking for. If I want them to coach to their full potential, I have to not only allow them to be authentically themselves but insist upon it.

When Lane Kiffin and Rocky Seto came aboard as young coaches in our first year at USC, they were surrounded by a variety of veterans—all fiery, tough coaches whose energy was infectious. As Lane and Rocky were developing, they watched those coaches and observed how hard they were on their players. Predictably, Lane and Rocky both began to coach hard themselves, with a demeanor that didn't necessarily fit their personalities. They would yell and scream, but it was evident to me that they were acting outside themselves. After a few weeks, I sat down with each of them individually to discuss their approach.

We discussed how they were coaching outside their personalities and how that would weaken them in the long run. For them to maximize their players' ability, I explained, they would have to teach from inside themselves, because that was what would make them the most authentic and effective coaches possible. They listened to my advice and it was a blast after that to watch Lane and Rocky develop each season into more efficient teachers and more confident coaches. As the two of them grew up within our system, they worked to develop their own personal coaching style.

Ultimately, the most critical point in coaching our coaches is to understand that we don't want every coach to have the same style. What we need on our staff are unique competitors who can each find a way to deliver the same message with one heartbeat. The coaches need to internalize the message and then convey it in their own voice. When each person does that, we get a diversity of styles and approaches that makes the whole team stronger.

Putting together a staff may be the most important part of any head coach's job, and I have always enjoyed it. I am often asked what I look for when hiring coaches. The first thing I look at is a person's competitiveness and work ethic. I also like to hire young and promote from within. There have been exceptions along the way, of course, but for the most part I would rather get someone who is open-minded and full of competitive fire, even if it comes at the expense of a certain amount of experience.

You can teach people how to coach football and the nuances of the game. It is no secret, after all, that I have basically been running the same defense I learned from Monte Kiffin in the 1970s—and who knows how long he had been running it before then. Specific plays aren't what made all those USC victories, and they aren't necessarily what are going to power the Seahawks. Perhaps the most powerful weapon in the Win Forever philosophy is the drive to constantly be looking for ways to improve. That mentality makes a huge difference when I'm looking to hire coaches for my staff.

The other critical factor we look for when hiring new coaches is their willingness and ability to grow. Leadership development is critical in any organization. One person at the top simply can't do everything that needs to be done. You need a head coach who has the ultimate authority and responsibility, but his job is a lot more fun and the team is a lot stronger if he has other smart, capable leaders around him. And it is his job to develop them.

If a leader is clear and consistent about his philosophy's core values, it frees everyone up to do their best. It frees the top leadership to treat its middle managers in a whole new way. When everyone understands the vision, the goals, and the overall system, they don't need the top boss always telling them what to do. They can figure it out for themselves. And for the middle managers, this means that instead of being mere instruments for relaying instructions delivered from on high, they can get creative and share their own ideas. Once they have the chance to find their own voices, their identity is now at the forefront. The door then opens to competing not merely for the next promotion but to maximize their own potential. Imagine how much energy this generates. When everyone gets to contribute his maximum effort, it is transformative for the whole organization.

In Los Angeles, there is plenty of glory as well as scrutiny surrounding the USC program; most of that attention is focused on the players and head coach. It is intensified by the fact that there is a huge media market with no NFL franchise for fans to focus on. However, it was the assistant coaches who were the unsung heroes of our team.

Our coaching staff was the heartbeat of our program for nine years. The ultimate responsibility stopped with me, but it was their constant contact with the players that provided the leadership, set the tone, and carried the message to our team. They did all this with a level of enthusiasm, competition, and ownership that generated excitement and drive.

Inevitably in sports—and in business as well—you hear a lot of talk about star players and the leadership they provide, as if their position coaches were somehow merely support staff. Most coaches think that leadership comes from the players, but I don't see it that way. The leadership that I count on most comes from our coaches.

Developing leadership in players is instrumental on any team, but it is not always something that you can depend on, especially at the high school or college level. You want to compete with people you can trust to lead and those are my coaches. Our efforts to win are based on our ability to control every aspect of our team environment, from energy to focus to camaraderie. When the team's natural chemistry takes the form we want, that's an added advantage we're happy to have, but we cannot afford to hang our success on the hope that this will happen. A player, however talented, may have a bad day. Something may have happened in his family, or he may be under the weather or down on himself for a variety of reasons. Leadership the team can depend on must be consistent and stable to be most effective. The only leadership that I can really rely on is that which comes from our coaching staff. The coaches are constantly nurturing our players' abilities to serve as part of the team's leadership. But it is the coaches that I hold accountable. You can try to position and promote players in ways that make them leaders, but I don't want to rely on them when it comes to winning or losing. I have chosen to rely on our staff first and foremost.

Just as our football players do everything to prepare for practice, our coaches do the same. For instance, there's a staff meeting I like to have with all of my position coaches before the start of spring practice. At the meeting, they are asked to deliver to the entire staff the speech they are going to give at their first players' meeting. I've always thought it's really important to have a great first meeting with each position group, so at USC we came up with a way to practice that. I made it clear that I put a lot of value on these meetings, so the guys spent a lot of time preparing their speeches before we all got together.

At the conclusion of each person's presentation, the rest of the staff critiqued it and offered coaching on content, delivery, props, performance, anything else we noticed that could help him do a better job. We filmed each presentation for him to be able to review, just as a player reviews his practice film. The two major areas we critiqued were how true each coach was to the approach of the program, and how authentic he was to his own personality and style. As long as the coaches satisfied these two criteria, they were encouraged to be as creative and entertaining in their delivery as they could. Invariably, the coaches who exuded the most passion and sincerity had the best results.

These coaches were tough, competitive guys, so it wasn't always easy for them to be evaluated in front of their peers like that. The fact that we did it showed how committed we were to improving and how seriously we took that effort. It was a very productive exercise for a couple of reasons. For one thing, they usually got a lot of good tips and suggestions from the other coaches. For another, it let them see how their colleagues operated, and also just how impressive, and how different from one another they really were.

Some had elaborate PowerPoint presentations to go with their speeches, and some worked off notes written on crumpled pieces of paper that they pulled out of their back pockets. Some were loud and boisterous, using colorful language, while others were more reserved and businesslike. But no matter the style of their presentations, each coach seemed to capture the room's attention and delivered his speech in his own unique way.

Whether in football or in business, there is so much more room for personal style and expression than many people realize. Whatever the context, not taking advantage of that may be a huge missed opportunity to involve people on a deeper, more competitive, and ultimately higher-performing level. How can an organization expect to maximize its overall potential if its people up and down the ladder don't have the chance to contribute in a way that taps into their ability as individuals? What if managers and bosses thought of themselves as coaches instead? What if leaders in other professions saw their jobs not just in terms of getting the most production out of their people, but in terms of teaching their workers to become the best they can be?

The flip side of hiring a coaching staff made up of great competitors with strong voices of their own is that sooner or later they're going to move on. And often it is sooner. High turnover rates are something I have learned to not only accept but embrace. At USC our staff was composed of mostly young, ambitious coaches who were in the process of building great careers. I was eager for them to do well. It is one of the things that make a Win Forever organization dynamic. So rather than expecting loyalty from my coaches, I found that I got all the loyalty I could ask for by supporting them and advancing their careers.

Of course, sometimes loyalty goes even further than that. I was lucky enough to have my son Brennan on our staff for several years. He started as a graduate assistant and eventually moved on to become a full-time coach and recruiting coordinator. He joined the staff at the start of my second year, and the experience ended up being beneficial to both of us. Brennan grew up with football but had never planned on being a coach. Transitioning into this new opportunity, though, I really felt I needed the voice of someone so close to me whom I could trust, so he agreed to come on board. Brennan has always had a high-spirited, smart personality, so I knew exactly what we'd be getting—a loyal competitor with a strong work ethic. And he was a real asset for us. There's nothing more exciting than to compete at a high level alongside a member of your family. I don't know how many people get to do that. At the same time, with Brennan there I felt like there was always someone who was watching out for me. He always shot straight with me, and I really respect him and am grateful for his commitment. Without him it would never have been the same.

Not all new coaches are going to know me that well, however, so I make every effort to ensure that the coaches understand where I am coming from. Even from the first conversations with prospective coaches, I make sure they know that I am invested in their long-term success and that I will do everything I can so that they can get the job of their dreams. So while I am their "boss," I am cognizant of being their "coach" as well. Getting involved in their careers beyond the team is one way for me to do that. I talk to our staff about their long-term career ambitions on a regular basis, and we even go so far as to stage mock interviews for the types of positions they're hoping for down the road.

I believe that our coaches should get everything that they want out of their association with our program, and I'll work with them to accomplish that. I want that understood before they even come on board and that's the opportunity they'll have with us.

Not that all of this is self-sacrificing—far from it. There are several competitive benefits to our approach to staff attrition. I want to create an atmosphere that is beneficial to the coaches who come through our doors and when someone leaves, we have other applicants competing to fill the job. Everyone wins in that scenario. For the same reasons great players come to USC in hopes of being drafted into the NFL, coaches come to USC knowing that they could one day be in the running for coordinator and head coaching jobs in the college or professional ranks.

Sometimes we would lose a great player after his third season; sometimes a coach would get a great offer and leave us sooner than we would have liked. These are just facts of life in our world, and since we can't change them we look for ways to make them work for us. I always try to look at this as an opportunity: When a player leaves, that creates an opportunity for the next guy, and the same goes for our coaching staff. We always want to have people in reserve ready to step in as openings arise.

This element of a Win Forever program is a simple truth about the nature of competition. We're only going to Win Forever if we can build a staff of people who are constantly competing to reach their full potential—and part of that is the pursuit of their own career ambitions. As we are constantly saying, you're either competing or you're not, but how that competitive thought takes shape is unique to each person.

Due to the hours we work, and the commitment and goals we share, a Win Forever organization is a very tight community. Our success depends on every one of us being willing to sacrifice parts of ourselves to the shared effort. That only works when we trust one another completely, and once that level of trust is in place, it's worth a lot to keep it there. No matter how professional a coach may be, if he feels like he is being stifled or not being treated fairly in the program, it is likely to challenge his ability to perform.

For all these reasons, I want our guys to know that we believe in them, and I want to show them how far we will go to stand by them. When I do that, I get it back many times over in the long run. In my own career, there have been a couple of times when teams I worked for said they would support me when the time came but didn't. I've never forgotten that, and I don't want my guys ever to feel that way.

One such experience came in the late 1980s when I was coaching the defensive backs at the Minnesota Vikings. I had been there for several years, when a similar position opened up in San Francisco. Although I was technically still under contract, we had always been told that whenever we wanted to go somewhere else, we would get permission to leave. But when I went to the head coach, he told me that he didn't think it was the right job for me and that my career would be better off where I was. When I pressed, explaining that I wanted to find out more about the job—among other reasons, because it was a chance to go back to my hometown—he flat-out refused to let me go.

The next year, going into my last contract year in Minnesota, the general manager offered a bonus of ten thousand dollars to anyone who signed a two-year deal, as long as the team made it to the play-offs that season. At the time I wasn't making a big-time salary, so that was really a lot of money. Even so, I was still upset over the previous year and decided that no amount of money was worth giving up my free agency.

Sure enough, we made the play-offs that year by winning our final game against Cincinnati, and as we were sitting in the coaches' box watching the clock run down, Monte leaned over to me with a piece of paper in his hand with "$10,000" written on it. He crossed the figure out and then handed it to me as a joke. I actually laughed pretty hard at the time as I said, "Thanks, Monte." While I was not happy being out the money, I did have my freedom. At the end of the season, I received an offer to become the New York Jets defensive coordinator, and I was gone. It's not as if I made any enemies over the incident, but the whole thing left me with a sense of how I would run things if I ever got the chance. Obviously, I was learning that having the freedom to weigh my options was more important to me than money or a sense of security.

In Seattle, as at USC, I want everyone to know that we want them to realize their dreams. I want people who will fight for us because they know we'll fight for them. The idea of holding someone back just because they can help us in the short term is not only totally contrary to the spirit of our philosophy, it's self-defeating. I want everyone in our organization to maximize their potential, and I'll compete as hard as I can to make that happen.

13

COACHES ARE TEACHERS

We live in a society that celebrates executives, coaches, and other "leaders" yet doesn't put a very high value on teaching as a profession. But any successful leader will tell you that leading and teaching go hand in hand. In Win Forever terms, you really can't be a leader if you're not a great teacher.

It will be no surprise by now when I say that, like everything else in my life, I approach teaching as a competition. As a coach, I am competing to teach each player as effectively as I possibly can, so that he can become the best possible player for our team.

A coach's job is to build winning teams, and we use everything at our disposal to get that done. That's why I've never understood why so many coaches take a rigid, one-size-fits-all approach when it comes to their leadership style. The way I see it, if it were that easy everyone would be able to do it, and being a great coach and leader would no longer be a competitive lifestyle.

What many people fail to realize is that flexible and open communication is an incredibly powerful leadership tool. It is through effective communication that we are able to reach the ultimate goal of helping others perform at their very best. To Win Forever as an organization, we must find a way to approach each unique individual in a manner that maximizes his or her potential.

I have seen firsthand so many situations where the coach and his athlete just couldn't communicate and the relationship faltered. To me, failure to communicate is unacceptable for a parent, a coach, or a leader. It is easy to get frustrated when we see someone we are responsible for fail to make progress, and especially frustrating when we see a lack of effort. As parents, it is our responsibility to find avenues to communicate with our children, and it's the same for a coach or leader. We are the ones in charge, and we must accept the accountability associated with that. We are the ones with something to communicate, so it is up to us to figure out how to communicate it effectively to the person we want to learn it. As parents and coaches, it is up to us to compete to find ways to connect with our children and players.

One of the most important principles in our approach to being effective teachers is to strive to develop a deep understanding of each individual student or player. Every player in our program is a unique individual from a specific background, and before we can effectively reach and connect with him we must develop a relationship. Then we must formulate an approach that will enable the teaching and learning process. Therefore, one of the coaching mantras around our program at USC and now in Seattle is to "learn your learner."

The competitive environment we operate in as coaches demands that we be extraordinary teachers. We have no choice but to go to great lengths to uncover the most effective ways to get to know our players. One of the most obvious but productive methods is through consistent and watchful observation. We can glean a wealth of information by paying close attention to the actions, mannerisms, and traits of our players. By taking note of the clothes they wear, the hairstyles they choose, their personal interests, and the people they choose to hang out with, we get mountains of information. For example, when players arrived at USC, our academic support group would begin formal and informal diagnostics for learning styles and aptitudes. We shared and exchanged information to create a profile that would accurately direct our efforts to teach each player successfully.

We wanted to observe our players in as many situations and scenarios as possible. We needed to see them in their comfort zones as well as outside their comfort zones. For instance, when we attended the Manhattan Beach Volleyball Open during each training camp, our staff was constantly evaluating our players throughout the afternoon, learning about them off the field.

It's a challenge to understand the people you're dealing with so that you can approach them in the most effective possible way—a way that allows them to operate and perform at their very best. But it's a battle you need to wage if you are serious about helping people be the best that they can be.

That's why I work so hard to instill in my coaching staff the importance of learning your learner. A teacher, coach, or manager who knows his learner is able to accurately communicate in a manner that best suits that learner, and the more effectively a leader can communicate his or her expectations, the better the results are going to be.

In terms of learning your learners, no one has had more of an effect on me over the years than Coach Bud Grant back in Minnesota. He was a master at this and would concoct all types of opportunities to observe his players and learn the extent to which they had really gotten the message. He had an extraordinary awareness of the signals people gave off and understood how to use that information to spur them to play at their best possible level.

In this way, Coach Grant was one of the people who most influenced me to broaden my perspective on what matters and what doesn't. He taught me to use my peripheral vision, so to speak, to observe my players at every opportunity. He taught me that if you learn to become a good watcher and listener, you'll be rewarded with a wealth of information that you can use to compete more successfully. I learned from him that the best teachers, coaches, and leaders are often the best observers. Watching and, in particular, listening intently is crucial. So much of my job is about communicating outwardly to others, but I am able to do that effectively because I have disciplined myself to be a focused listener. I take great pride in that because it is no easy task.

I remember one occasion in particular when I was the defensive backs coach at the Vikings and Bud was head coach. It was the very first day of fall training camp, and Bud had sent the players out on a long-distance run circling the field. For most coaches—including me at the time—that would have been a chance for some downtime, and that's how we were treating it. I recall standing on the edge of the field jabbering with one of my fellow coaches, when I saw Coach Grant glaring at me. "Pete! What the hell is the matter with you?" he snapped. "You're not watching!"

Watching what? I thought to myself. To me, that distance run was nothing more than a conditioning exercise, nothing to pay any particular attention to other than maybe noticing who came in first. But to Bud that simple exercise was an open book from start to finish. In the patterns of who was out ahead, who stayed in the cluster, who slowed down or sped up relative to their positions among the rest of the group, he saw as deeply into those players' competitive natures as any psychologist could. And that knowledge gave him an edge when it came to figuring out how to deal with each of them. Coach knew better than anyone that we were training football players, not marathon runners, but that wasn't the point. The point was to create a situation where he could watch and learn about his players' competitive natures. The indelible lesson was that everything counts. I've never forgotten it.

Coach Grant also had a terrific sense of humor to go along with that intuition and would use it to make more observations about his players. At times he would put out signs in random places that said "Keep off the Grass," just to see who would do what the sign said. He had a rule that everyone had to wear collared shirts at dinner when we were on the road for away games. Coach couldn't have cared *less* whether or not people wore collared shirts at dinner—he just wanted to see who would and who wouldn't. It was a way for him to learn just a little bit more.

Although at that point in my career I was still far from being able to put that sentiment into words, Coach Grant's example radically broadened my understanding of what it meant to truly compete. His keen insight into human behavior taught me the importance of not drawing a line between the places where you compete and the places where you don't. Because really, that line doesn't exist: You're either competing at everything or you're not.

In the spring of 2009, I was on our practice field at USC watching the offense run through a variety of plays. It was not a perfect practice, and a couple of players were not giving great effort. Our offensive coordinator at the time, John Morton, could sense it, and he called up the entire offense. He expressed his disapproval of their effort and demanded that they work harder with a greater focus—and that's a polite way of saying he ripped into them.

As they continued to practice, I pulled John aside and asked him to think about what he was really trying to achieve. While I didn't disagree with his actions, I asked him if he realized that the vast majority of the offense was working hard and that he had just hollered at everyone because of two players' actions. Right away, he understood. Sometimes, when confronted with a problem, simply taking the time to assess the situation will often determine the best response.

Every year, before the start of spring and fall practice, I would remind our staff that players will all make mistakes and that in the window of a few seconds after a particular mistake, we make the choice between yelling at the player or helping him learn from his missed assignment. It is in those few seconds that coaches can have the most impact. Resisting the impulse to respond in a negative way is one of the biggest challenges coaches face.

Early in my coaching career at UOP, I experienced how important communication could be. In a critical moment, in the middle of a hard-fought game, I was disappointed with a decision a freshman player had made on a particular play, and I decided to correct it on the spot. As he approached the sidelines, I blurted out a few of those emotional, obscenity-laden, lost-in-the-moment phrases: "Hey, Brian, what the heck were you thinking out there? What are you trying to do, lose the game?" It certainly was not very classy, even in the heat of the battle. Brian, however, was a very bright and thoughtful kid, who went on to play for a number of years in the NFL for, ironically, the Seattle Seahawks. Until that moment we'd had a very good relationship. But now all of that was set aside. Here was a young kid trying to decipher for himself what had happened on the field, and a coach he trusted had come unglued and was yelling obscenities at him. He looked at me and simply said: "Why are you asking me like that?"

His question hit me square between the eyes. What was I trying to do, undermine that young man's self-confidence in the heat of battle? Later it dawned on me that I had misdirected the focus of the moment to a personal confrontation that did nothing to help us win the game, and it had happened because of my tone of voice and choice of language. I see it now as a colossal blunder on my part. It's hard enough to perform at your best with everything fully functioning and in focus. My players didn't need me making it harder. I had learned a valuable lesson about the power of effective communication in a heated, competitive setting. I will never forget what Brian taught me that day, and since then I have tried my best to make sure that all my communication is measured and calculated precisely to maximize the moment.

As the years passed, I would find myself asking coaches who worked for me, "If self-confidence is so important, why would we ever want to approach someone in a manner that might disrupt or shatter it?" I am absolutely certain that our awareness of communication, particularly in the heat of battle, has accounted for more than a few of our wins along the way.

The major coaching point here is the power of language and communication skills. It is important to only use language that facilitates the message and promotes the desired performance. Harsh language can be very effective if the situation and the audience can benefit from it. Sometimes raw emotion is the critical message to convey, and raw language can effectively facilitate the exchange. There are plenty of examples in my football experience where the single most important message that needed to be conveyed was simply an intense, blood-and-guts plea for a relentless explosion of courage and effort. No time for questions, no time for plans, the time is now and "we have got to have it" type of language may be called for. The coach relays his message because duty calls, and the response must be automatic. But some coaches think that at times like this, anything goes. That is not only wrong but also shows a loss of focus on what is important. You have to remember that high-level performance is what you are trying to attain.

There are people who say that you can't simultaneously maintain discipline and have open, accessible lines of communication between different levels of an organization. That's just not true. It has always been important to me to have a solid line of communication with my players and coaches. I never want to be cut off from the flow of what's going on and what everybody is thinking. I want to have the pulse of the group at all times. Therefore, open communication in all directions has always been important to me.

To maintain the flow of information, I need to be available at all times. So my door is always open and I'm watching and listening to stay in constant contact with my team. This is why we spend so much time together, going to a variety of events and sharing experiences in small groups and as a team. The art of creating an environment of open communication is of paramount importance to me. For instance, at USC, once in a while on Monday nights our quarterbacks would come up to the office and we would watch *Monday Night Football* together. We would hang out, have fun, and share stories about whatever came up in the game. In that time I would be getting to know our signal callers and they would be getting to know me in a casual setting. I was competing to learn my learners in hopes of becoming a better teacher.

There is extraordinary value in knowing your people, and it is worth the investment of your time. For me, this effort to know more about our players is never ending, as our teaching is never ending.

Because I spend a good deal of time hanging out with our players—especially the quarterbacks, who spend the most time in the film room—a sense of familiarity grows, which ends up helping us on the field. Sometimes, I have been called a "players' coach," which is a label that carries some negative connotations, such as being too nice or too close to the players. It doesn't bother me at all. It is through the strength of my relationships with my players that I gain insight into how to guide and challenge them to be their best. If you really care about helping people maximize their potential, then you must try to uncover who they are and what they are all about.

One quarterback we were able to develop with great results at USC, in large part through the strength of that relationship, was Mark Sanchez.

Mark was a beacon in our program from the day he arrived on campus. He embodied everything a Trojan should be. Mark was humble as a backup during his first three seasons, playing behind John David Booty. He led our program as well as any signal caller we have had as a full-time starter, finishing with a 12-1 record, 3,207 passing yards, and thirty-four touchdowns. He guided us to a Rose Bowl victory over Penn State, when he threw for 413 yards and four touchdowns. His performance set him up to have a senior season similar to Carson Palmer and Matt Leinart, and he would have been a front-runner for the Heisman Trophy the following year.

But as other quarterbacks around the nation began to announce their plans to return for their senior seasons, it opened up the door for Mark to be one of the top rated quarterbacks in the 2009 NFL draft. As we did with all of our players, we gained all the necessary information from NFL sources to assist Mark with his decision. We were told that he would be a top-fifteen pick and would have to have a great work out and interview to move into the top ten. I knew Mark would work out extremely well and would be impressive in his interviews, but he was taking a risk in entering the draft early. Many NFL teams were not high on rookie quarterbacks, and signal callers who had entered the draft after their junior year had not done well in recent NFL history.

After days of discussion, finally, on the night before the announcement of his decision, we had a late-night chat over In-N-Out burgers and I gave Mark and his family my advice—return for his senior year and leave USC competing to possibly be the first pick in the NFL draft, just like Carson Palmer, Mark's childhood idol.

Within twelve hours of our final discussion, Mark made his decision—and not the one I'd been hoping for. He was going to forgo his senior season and apply for the NFL draft. In his press conference, much was made of my opinion, as I stated that he was going against my advice by leaving early. Yet while we disagreed fundamentally, my opinion was based on the facts I had learned about the NFL during my time there and the information that was passed along to Mark and me by NFL scouts. I felt that as a starter for only sixteen games, he was taking a big chance by leaving early and would not get the return for all his hard work to get to this point.

While it was perceived in that press conference that Mark and I had a strained relationship, we have actually become closer as a result of the experience. He understood where I was coming from as an adviser, and I understood where he was coming from as a competitor. Mark wanted to fulfill his lifelong dream of playing quarterback in the NFL, and I just wanted him to have a better guarantee of future success. I would have advised my own son exactly the same way. But I love that he stayed with his belief in himself and proved his decision to be the right one for him.

Fortunately, the New York Jets made Mark the fifth player taken in the 2009 NFL draft, and he went on to find the success we had hoped for. He started as a rookie and set an all-time rookie record by winning his first three games. Though there were some bumps along the way, he eventually led his team to the AFC championship game. While he doesn't regret leaving early and I don't regret disagreeing with him, we both wish that the press conference had not come across as negatively as it did. We remain close, and while I was at USC, we talked periodically during the season to check in about his recent games and how our Trojans were playing. Now, getting to battle in the same league as Mark and so many of our former USC players, it will not only be exciting but will make for great fun.

Whether great competitors are born or made is an interesting question. I've found, though, that all aspiring champions—from young guys like Mark and Carson to legends like Jerry Rice—need coaching to help them reach their potential. I believe the greatest competitors of our time own a deep-down desire to be the best. They are driven to constantly prove and validate their greatness. Even though competitive levels vary from person to person, I believe that competition is something that can be taught and learned.

In our program, we believe that if you want to help someone be the best he can be, you have to learn as much as possible about what makes him tick. Our staff at USC, and now in Seattle, understands that we have to be open to the competitive idea that *everything* a player does is an opportunity for us to learn something about him. I'm reminded of Coach Grant's belief that to be a successful coach you need to be a great observer and a great listener.

14

OUR APPROACH TO PRACTICE

"Practice is Everything" is one of the core tenets of the Win Forever philosophy. We want to create an environment that will permit each of our players to reach his maximum potential, and one of the ways we do that is by practicing with great focus. A player who is fully prepared on the practice field will feel ready to meet whatever comes his way on game day and thus, feel more confident and able to minimize distractions of fear or doubt.

As coaches, we want to run a practice regimen that continually covers all the fundamentals of sound football but varies enough to prepare the team for all contingencies and keep the players' attention. This is not easy to accomplish, but it is a challenge that our staff embraces. We want to develop an environment that fosters learning and develops confidence.

Our goal is to consistently be the most effective football team we can be. When game day comes along, we want to be fully prepared. We don't want to be worried about anything. We just want to cut loose, let it rip, and be ourselves. Having a routine can be very powerful in this regard. If you compete day in and day out to excel at something in a systematic way, you can't help but improve. While we are always making small adjustments according to what we need to work on at a particular time, the basic structure and routines of our practices are totally consistent. Beginning with the team meeting and ending with the final play of practice, the details of each day's work are accounted for down to the minute.

At USC, we began each practice day with a team meeting. There, I always attempted to set the focus and tone for the day, always with enthusiasm. I was simply demonstrating the energy I wished to see from the coaches and players as we approached practice that day. We tried to keep these meetings short so that when the team broke up into position groups, the coaches had time to cover the assignments for the day in more detail. A primary job of the position coaches, however, was to reinforce the level of excitement and enthusiasm. The energy and the spirit of the day was paramount.

During the first few minutes of most team meetings we would talk about daily events going on around the world, both in sports and outside them. We would make general announcements and try to capture everyone's attention as we began to focus on the day. My goal was to create a close-knit environment, with our coaches and players sharing responsibility for the day's outcome.

We also showed highlights from the previous day's practice. The players didn't know which plays were going to go up on the big screen, but they did know that if they had been dogging it, that play would surely be shown, accompanied by hooting and hollering. The coaches had a blast with it, and there were always funny plays that we showed back and forth in slow motion. But the very serious belief remained: "Practice is Everything." By beginning each meeting with highlights, we energized the atmosphere, got the juices flowing, and had some fun jump-starting the day.

Our topics for the day might include areas we needed to work on or notable moments from practice the day before. We might call out someone's birthday or point out a notable academic accomplishment of one of our players. I loved to talk about sporting events and current national and world issues, especially if they could serve as educational moments. Another one of my favorite activities was to acknowledge and introduce notable visitors or former players who were on campus visiting the Trojans.

From a leadership perspective, these meetings were a great opportunity to connect. As a leader, I don't see any benefit in maintaining a reserve or keeping a distance, the way some other coaches did when I was growing up. I wanted our players to feel my enthusiasm and the coaching staff's enthusiasm and get geared up for the day. I wanted them to know that we cared and that the task ahead in practice was as much a chance for them to shine as any conference game. We spared no effort to make sure that our guys approached every practice as an opportunity and a challenge. I wanted them to see practice as something to look forward to with excitement and focus. When we did that properly, our practices were as competitive and fiery as any game.

Regardless of whatever we discussed or did in the team meeting, by the time we reached the practice field we were into serious business. Our players needed to channel the energy from the team meeting into an unshakably competitive state of mind so that they could take advantage of the practice opportunities.

Once practice began, everyone was expected to operate at full throttle. I wanted to practice at game speed. We would never allow for anything but full speed and full effort in games, and I wanted us to practice exactly like we played. I believe when you give athletes a chance to perform at varying levels of intensity, you offer an invitation for varying levels of performance. Once we transitioned from prepractice and team stretching to actual practice, I wanted everyone flying around the field. We liked to remind our players, "If you're walking, you're wrong!"

On-field practice was carefully scripted as a series of competitive events and situations, building step by step from the individual parts of the team to the whole. We would start with individual work, things like skill-developing drills, blocking and tackling, route running, throwing, and catching. From there we moved on through an ever-mounting series of one-on-one matchups, the wide receivers against the defensive backs, running backs versus the linebackers, offensive line against the defensive line, and so on, getting more and more players involved.

Playing and practicing with "great effort" was one of the hallmarks of our program. The position coaches would lead their groups, but the whole time the coordinators and I were running around the field from drill to drill, letting everyone know how closely we were watching their effort. One of the reminders for our coaches was to "critique effort first," meaning they were to look at the effort the players were demonstrating before critiquing assignments and techniques.

One of the ways we would heighten the atmosphere of competition was by making sure our players were matched up against the teammates who would challenge them the most. It's one thing for coaches to talk about how we expect players to compete, but it's another to put them in actual situations where they *must* compete. Our goal was for our players to face tougher opposition on our practice field than they would encounter in games. As we went through our practices, our best offense would match up against our best defense as much as possible. By pitting the best against the best we would force our players to maximize their potential in an environment we controlled.

We made a big deal out of these matchups. We wanted to raise the competitive bar as high as possible and create a "competitive cauldron." That's a phrase coined by Anson Dorrance, the legendary women's soccer coach at the University of North Carolina. If you don't follow soccer and haven't heard of him, Dorrance is one of the true coaching legends in sports. In thirty-one years as head coach at UNC, he has led his Tar Heels to twenty national championships. As of last season, his teams were 696-36-22 and he has set the bar in college soccer. Talk about Winning Forever!

Anson and I met for the first time in 2005, when both of us had the chance to visit the White House after our teams won national championships. I had been an admirer of his for years and had read his book long before I went to USC. What you want to do on the practice field, he wrote, is to create a "competitive cauldron" where the players are constantly in a gamelike state, competing for even the smallest wins. Instead of just doing drills, you keep score as much as possible. You make it so somebody wins and somebody loses.

After every practice, Dorrance's staff would post the scores of the day. Dorrance would watch to see how the players responded: Who would be driven to change and improve, and who would argue about whether the scores were fair? The actual results weren't so important. It was a way for him to drive home the point that you have to compete. You have to focus during every moment of practice or you'll get your butt kicked. There are no choices: you're either competing or you're not!

I adopted Dorrance's approach for a number of reasons. As a motivational tool, it helped us make sure the players were practicing at a very high level. If our overall job is helping our players be the best they can be, a huge part of that is orchestrating an environment where they are receptive to and ready for what we have to give them.

Keeping the competition at a fever pitch is an incredibly powerful tool in this regard.

No one wanted to be the one who got beaten, but unfortunately on our practice field that happened every day. We kept score during everything—one-on-ones, seven-on-seven passing drills, and our team period. We even created a scoring system. For instance, during seven-on-seven the offense got one point for a completion, while the defense was awarded two points for an incompletion. Either side could get three points on a touchdown pass or an interception.

During the team period, we would keep score in every way we could think of: first-and-ten situations, second-and-shorts, third-and-longs, and so on. We often varied what happened at the end as much as we could to keep things interesting and make those victories feel significant. Bragging rights were a given, and the guys loved to get after one another. We practiced with real officials, but even so, there were constant arguments over who had won each play. I loved it when the outcome of the overall practice came down to the last play of the day.

In 2002, on a mid-October afternoon, the energy of practice reached new heights on the Howard Jones Practice Field at USC. During our final team period of the day, our offense lined up in a pro set, one wide receiver on each side of the formation. As the ball was snapped, Carson Palmer handed it off to one of our running backs. Simultaneously, Sandy Fletcher, a receiver, took a direct path toward Troy Polamalu, our All-American safety and captain. Just as Troy was racing toward the ball carrier to make the tackle, Sandy appeared out of nowhere and absolutely blindsided Troy. It was a hit that made the offense run around and cheer wildly and one that stoked the defense's fire even more.

From that point on, Troy simply took over. He made every tackle, racing from one side of the field to the other, and not just getting in on every tackle but being sure to make his presence felt on every single snap. He was delivering crushing blows to running backs, dishing out forearm shivers to offensive guards and putting them on their backs, and doing it all with a look of extreme focus that made me somewhat concerned for the offensive players' safety. Troy was proving a point: *You may get me once when I'm not looking, but you will never get another shot like that.* It became such a scene on the practice field, as Troy was literally making every play, that I ended up calling practice early because we didn't want him or our other players to get hurt. Nonetheless, it was a great example of how intense it got from sideline to sideline on our practice field at USC.

We would always strive to create continuity and consistency. We were even very careful to be precise with our language and terminology. I don't like synonyms and varied definitions when it comes to terminology. If you want to communicate effectively, you need to be clear with the words you use.

We also recognized the need for a certain amount of variety. You cannot coach for very long without recognizing that routine, though necessary for success, can sometimes become monotonous.

Routine is enormously helpful in teaching players essential fundamentals. If you practice something consistently enough, when the critical moment comes in a game, the players will be able to perform without tightening up. They will be comfortable with the situation and make the right decisions. But if you believe in the importance of practice, as I do, you also know that you have to always keep your players interested and fully engaged. You can't just do the same thing practice after practice or the players will lose interest.

All coaches face this problem in one way or another. Too little routine and the message doesn't get through; too much, and your players can get worn out. Finding the right balance and emphasis is critical for keeping practices fresh and players focused.

The way we handled it at USC was to have a different theme for each day of the week during the season.

"Tell the Truth Monday" was the day when we got our entire team on the same page in terms of what had occurred in our last game. Who performed well and who didn't? Why did the game go as it did and what should we take away from this game experience? It was imperative on this day that we think and speak as one and move ahead in harmony.

We asked ourselves: Did we protect the football? Were we physical? Did our defense swarm to the football? If we had not accomplished our goals, we discussed why that had occurred and how to fix it. We had to address the issues, make corrections, and move on to the next game. It was always good for our players because they had been taught that the tape doesn't lie. As the years went on, Mondays were always great days for our program. They were when we plugged back into who we were and that enabled us to refocus for the week. After talking about the game, we would always show the players a few minutes of TV clips because they loved to hear the announcers and listen to the pageantry surrounding their performance.

Following the overview, the special teams coordinator would address each phase of the kicking game before the team broke into two groups, offense and defense. There, each respective coordinator would delve into greater detail of the truth about the past game. After breaking into specific position meetings to review game film, we would have an hour-long practice. There we would begin with a special teams segment followed by an introduction to our next opponent that involved practicing twenty plays against the base offensive and defensive looks we expected that week. We finished "Tell the Truth Monday" with twenty more plays of eleven on eleven where we split our squad into two groups. On one side of the field the starters on offense competed against the starters on defense, and on the other side of the field, the younger players practiced the same script as the upperclassmen.

I loved to observe the younger players, as this was a big day for them. It was also important for our younger coaches, as I would assign one on offense and one on defense to call the plays and act as the offensive and defensive coordinators. By doing that, we kept a high level of focus across the practice field and started the week off with great tempo.

Our staff would finish Monday by catching glimpses of *Monday Night Football*, usually cheering for one or more of our former players, while making recruiting calls and finalizing our base game plan for the week.

"Competition Tuesday" was the day we celebrated the central theme in the program—competition. We emphasized creating a great level of competition for the upcoming practice, with minimal attention paid to our opponent and the upcoming game. We accentuated the competitive matchups between individual players, position groups, and the offense and defense.

It all kicked off in our 9:00 A.M. staff meeting. There I would typically prod an assistant or two about competing. Sometimes I'd call out Ken Norton Jr. and his linebackers, who would be going up against Todd McNair and his running backs during the pass protection period, or get Pat Ruel riled up so he would get his offensive linemen to compete against Jethro Franklin's defensive line. While it may seem somewhat silly, each coach carried so much pride with his position group that he would bring the competitive mentality that I had fueled in the staff meeting earlier in the day to the team and individual position meetings.

In our team meeting we would sometimes have "matchups of the day," where I would ask a receiver whom he wanted to go against in one-on-ones and he would call out a cornerback, or a defensive line-man would call out an offensive tackle. Sometimes our coaches would call out one another, and that always jacked up the squad.

This was a lot of fun for everyone, but the beauty of Competition Tuesday was not only the one-on-one matchups but the focus it created on that particular day. Tuesday was our largest day of installation of the game plan and the most mentally taxing day of the week. By placing the focus on competition instead of the opponent, Competition Tuesday allowed us to direct our attention on getting better that day. It allowed them to remain focused on one play and one practice period at a time. Of course, we would be sure to play the film of each one of those matchups the next day in our meeting, and the amount of trash-talking among not only the players but the coaches was classic!

"Turnover Wednesday" was completely dedicated to the factor we believed most determines the outcome of football games, turnovers. USC won fifty-three straight games when we had a positive turnover ratio. Simply stated, when we created just one more turnover than our opponent, we were unbeatable. Long before this string was established, the first words out of my mouth when addressing our team each fall and each spring were always "It's All About the Ball!" I would follow that with a passionate presentation of how important the ball is in determining the outcomes of games. I reminded them that it is every player's number one responsibility to take care of the football accordingly.

If you're on offense, you do everything in your power to protect the football at all times—including the running backs, wide receivers, tight ends, and of course the decision maker, the quarterback. Even the offensive line must have an undying commitment to protect the ball at all times.

On defense, our sole objective was to get the ball. Every defensive call we made, every technique, every assignment, *everything* we did was designed to position our players to attack and get the ball from our opponents.

Turnover Wednesday was an entire day dedicated to taking care of and going after the football. On the practice field, Wednesday's competition was fixed on the ball. If the defense could get one turnover from the offense, they won that day. If the offense could secure the ball all day, with no interceptions and no fumbles lost, then they won that day. Spurred on by the coaches, this was a fierce competition all the way up to the final play in practice. It was an awesome day of the week on the field, but postpractice was almost as much fun.

Wednesday night was designated "Family Night" for our staff, and we had the opportunity to spend about thirty minutes hanging with our kids on the field throwing the football, playing games, and just having fun. It was great when the families could eat dinner together and get quality time with one another. The players also looked forward to this time when they could see their coaches' kids and understand the demands of this profession. They were always out on the field running around with the kids, enjoying themselves. That night was also our final night to make major game-plan adjustments, so when we walked out of the office we all had a good feeling heading into Thursday morning.

"No Repeat Thursday" was meant to emphasize the execution and precision of our weekly game plan. Practice was shorter on Thursday, with great focus on doing things right. All kicking game phases were emphasized along with a near-flawless demonstration of the game plan to such a precise level of performance that no plays needed to be repeated. Hence the name "No Repeat Thursday." I wanted to leave the practice field Thursday, our last workday of the week, knowing we were ready to perform at a championship level. I would do everything I could to convince our players they were worthy of "knowing" that they were ready to perform.

For coaches, Thursday was the greatest day of the week. Not only were the game plan and call sheet completed, but it was also their night off. Immediately after practice, the coaches would race to the locker room to quickly shower before heading home to see their kids, maybe have a "date night" with their wives, or just get away from work for a few hours. I'm a huge believer in balance, and as hard as it is to create during the season, we did our best to sneak away and be with our families for pockets of time. Being the head coach, I would typically be the last one to leave on Thursday, as I always wanted to see the practice film, but when I would get out of the office, I would hurry home to spend some time with my family.

"Review Friday" was our final on-field practice session and the last opportunity for all position groups to clean up issues and perfect their performance for game day. This was our most disciplined and regimented practice, where we paid strict attention to the fine details.

For our staff, Friday was all about proving to our players that they knew they were going to win and that we had earned the right to feel that way. We relied on our practice efforts during the week to lead us to this mentality, and we looked toward Review Friday to finalize the week.

The energy in the team meetings on Fridays was unparalleled. The players began the day with a variety of chants, songs, and dances. It was not always like this, but the run of championships bolstered the excitement in that room. We wanted to celebrate the upcoming weekend. Yet when we locked in and began to talk about the agenda for the day, the seriousness was palpable. It was usually less than twenty-four hours before kickoff.

If it was a home game, we'd have a pep rally in Heritage Hall after Friday's practice. It would be a relatively intimate setting, with the band, Song Girls, alumni, and fans in a room filled with championship plaques and Heisman Trophies. After a variety of songs, one of our assistants would climb up on a ladder and deliver a speech to the crowd. It was fun for our coaches because they got to deliver an inspirational message. More often than not it was something we had talked about in the staff room during the week. Always passionate and speaking from the heart, the coaches did a great job every week setting the tone for the pep rally. Following a few more songs, a senior player was called up to deliver a speech. This was always special, and I tried to make sure that each senior got an opportunity to speak to the crowd. For those players, our pep rally served as not only a fond memory but also an opportunity to become closer to the past Trojans who had stood on that same platform. This was something I always looked forward to and had a blast with and will surely miss in the NFL.

Following the pep rally, we would head to the team hotel in downtown Los Angeles. If it was an away game we would race from the practice field to the Los Angeles International Airport for an afternoon flight. Either way, we were in full pregame mode, with the special teams meeting that night at 7:30 P.M., offensive and defensive meetings after that, and finally a team meeting where I addressed the squad one last time before snack and bed check.

The point of everything that we did during the week and on Friday night was to get our players to a mental place where they knew they were going to win and to get them to believe that they did not have to do anything special once the ball was snapped. They only needed to trust their preparation and, as we said around USC, "let it rip." It was my responsibility to prove to them that they had earned the right to enjoy every moment of game day. All they needed to do was just go out and have fun playing football. In Seattle, we'll be playing our best football when that same confidence is acquired by our Seahawk players, and they can truly revel in playing the game they have known since they were kids. What better venue to perform in than Qwest Field, where the fans are among the loudest in the NFL.

The Howard Jones Practice Field at USC was where our players established their sense of themselves as individuals, as members of their position groups, as members of our offense or defense, and ultimately as part of the team as a whole. We used practice as an opportunity to cultivate both competition and cohesion at every level of the organization. Far from viewing it as a prelude to the main event on game day, our staff treated every practice as an individual event in and of itself, and we will do the same thing with the Seahawks.

As a football program, practice played a unique role for us that may not translate directly to the concerns of the rest of the world, but I believe that there are elements of our approach that can benefit anyone. There is no replacement for hard work and nothing that can take the place of competition.

15

FOURTH AND NINE

One of the aspects of our USC program that drew a lot of comments from the media was that on most days we opened our practices to the public. This is a policy that will continue during training camp in Seattle.

In the often paranoid, guarded world of high-level football, the inner workings of most teams are treated more like government secrets than public spectacles, but to me opening up our practices was a clear outgrowth of our "relentless pursuit of a competitive edge."

Having a crowd watch us practice was just one more way of helping our guys to prepare. Spectators are just another variable in the game. Players need to focus, no matter what is going on around them. We competed in front of an audience in our games, so why not practice in front of one? I never wanted to miss a single opportunity to simulate gamelike situations during practice. We wanted to do everything in our power to avoid encountering anything for the first time during a game. Many teams will set up speakers blasting the sounds of a packed stadium crowd, and we did that as well when preparing for games on the road. But there's something special about having real people there.

Having a crowd at practice served us better than keeping the environment quiet. Granted, it wasn't like having ninety thousand fans in the Los Angeles Memorial Coliseum on game day, but it still felt like we were performing—especially when there was a big turn-out. There was nothing better than an afternoon on Howard Jones Practice Field with the Trojan faithful on the sideline, with Art Bartner leading the Spirit of Troy marching band on an adjacent field. The energy was awesome and the atmosphere was festive, a fun exhibition of college football.

More often than not, we would have hundreds of people watching practice the week before a big game, and since we were in Los Angeles, sometimes that crowd would include a celebrity or two. I loved to have fun with our visitors whenever I could. It was a way of elevating and motivating our players to compete and perform to their fullest, instead of treating it as just another day running plays. We wanted to create a special environment that would enhance our performance.

This cut both ways, of course—although not necessarily in the way you might think. Just as in a real game, sometimes we would have a practice where for one reason or another we simply weren't functioning the way we should. Everyone has days like that, and we were no exception. Just as in a real game, the audience was going to see that, and our players were going to have to figure out how to deal with it. When we had a practice like that, it would have been easy to worry that having an audience might further shake our confidence and throw off our game even more. But I didn't see it that way.

Other people might have worried: *There are reporters out there—what are they going to write about us tomorrow? Will it shake us even more? Will it give our opponents an edge on game day?* But this couldn't be further from our attitude. What the coaches and I were seeing was a unique and fantastic teachable moment. We would not only acknowledge it, but we would embrace it to the point where we would call as much attention to the situation as we possibly could. If a practice was going wrong for some reason, I would call a simulated halftime and take the whole team off the field right there in front of everyone.

When we left the field, we'd create a mock locker room atmosphere. We'd get the team together and tell them to imagine that we were down 21–7 and that we needed to get "right" so we could go back out there and regain control of the game. Suddenly, a mediocre practice became a unique opportunity to learn how to remedy a poor performance. Far from embarrassing us, having that crowd there to see whether or not we could pull it off only made the moment that much more authentic, and the teachable moment that much more effective.

By making our practices competitive, by making the most of teachable moments, and by creating a stadium-like atmosphere, our players definitely felt more comfortable in real game situations. We couldn't have been more prepared, as we headed to South Bend, Indiana, to face Notre Dame, in what would become an epic game during the 2005 season. Both teams battled throughout the contest with the lead changing hands several times. Well into the third quarter, the outcome was still undecided and the atmosphere was electric, primed for the fourth quarter.

It is the game's final moments that are best remembered, but before either team took the field it was clear that the stage was set for a formidable battle between two great football teams. It was a classic USC–Notre Dame matchup. Our squad entered the game riding a twenty-seven-game winning streak, while Notre Dame was poised to end that streak with a victory that would validate Charlie Weis, their new head coach, as the real deal. We were playing at South Bend, and 80,795 Notre Dame fans had turned out with the intention to witness the moment when things turned around for their program. Notre Dame had done a fantastic job of riling their fans, pulling out all the stops by bringing in alums like Joe Montana and other past Irish greats to get them fired up. They even took the field in their trademark good-luck green jerseys. The atmosphere was awesome!

With 2:02 left in the game, it looked like they were going to get their wish when Notre Dame quarterback Brady Quinn dashed around our defensive end for a five-yard touchdown, to put them ahead 31–28. We took the ensuing kickoff back to our twenty-four-yard line, needing a field goal to tie, or a touchdown to win, and we only had 1:58 remaining on the clock.

The crowd was going absolutely berserk as our offense took the field. They were as loud as a jam-packed stadium could be, and when we threw an incomplete on the first play, they got even louder. Matt was sacked for a nine-yard loss on second down and I can honestly say the place was as loud as any stadium I had ever been in. On third and nineteen, if there had been a noise meter, I think it would have shattered.

We called a time-out and told Matt that we only needed to get half of the yardage back, knowing we would go for it on fourth down. We called an option route for Reggie Bush and he gained ten yards. That route, which Matt had thrown to Reggie countless times in practice, got us to fourth and nine at our own twenty-five-yard line. With 1:32 left on the clock we called our final time-out. We decided on a play that would hit tight end Dominique Byrd for a first down. The offensive coaches reminded Matt to be ready for the blitz. If the Irish lined up for a blitz, he would have to change the play.

Matt went back in the huddle to call the play. It was fourth down and Notre Dame was one play away from upsetting USC. The crowd was hostile, and as our team broke the huddle, the stadium got louder. Matt got under center and scanned the defense, seeking the one key that would force him to audible. As luck would have it, the Irish gave him the blitz look. Suddenly, in the most demanding environment you could possibly imagine, Matt had to call the audible and change not only the play but the entire pass protection and the receivers' routes. Matt barked out his cadence as the linemen relayed the audible. "Red 82 Stay, Red 82 Stay," yelled Matt, then "Go!" as he took the snap. This is a moment worth fully comprehending—if any of the ten other players failed to hear the audible that changed the play, the game might have been over. Near flawless execution was necessary for us to have a chance to get a first down and extend the game.

With the defense blitzing, Matt calmly took his five-step drop, as he had done countless times in practice, and lofted a picture-perfect pass down the left sideline to Dwayne Jarrett. As if in slow motion, somehow the ball found its way past the outstretched arms of a Notre Dame defender and into Dwayne's. All of a sudden, there was silence in Notre Dame Stadium as Dwayne sprinted down the sideline with only the goal line in front of him. It was one of the most exhilarating moments I've ever felt on a football field. Considering the circumstances, this was a historic play, but very simply, what actually occurred was a result of our preparation, which allowed every player to perform brilliantly under the most pressure-filled situation imaginable.

It looked like Dwayne was going to run for a touchtown, which would have put us ahead, but Notre Dame's cornerback managed a desperate dive, catching him by the heel and bringing him down on the thirteen-yard line. That fourth down play, in the most difficult of circumstances and with so much at stake, will always stick in my mind as a perfect illustration of our preparation and execution.

Still down 31–28, we were now in field-goal range, so it was all about clock management. With a little over a minute remaining, we called a pass to Steve Smith that fell incomplete. Consecutive runs by Reggie Bush brought us to the two-yard line with no time-outs and the clock quickly ticking down, 0:19, 0:18, 0:17, 0:16, 0:15.

We called for an empty backfield, as we had no choice but to throw into the end zone, either to score or stop the clock. As Matt dropped back, he could not find an open receiver, so he scrambled to his left, still scanning the field. He decided to tuck the ball and leap for the end zone, but as he got hit in midair, he fumbled the ball. An alert sideline official stopped the clock determining that the ball had gone out of bounds, leaving just seconds on the clock.

In the ensuing pandemonium, the Notre Dame players, coaches, fans, and scoreboard operator did not recognize that Matt had fumbled the ball and watched as the clock ticked down to zero. In unison, the players, coaches, alumni, and fans all rushed the field thinking they had just ended our winning streak. A member of the officiating crew quickly informed me that the clock had stopped with seven seconds remaining, and I knew that we had another chance at the end zone.

After the officials cleared the field, our players got into their huddle. During the mayhem I was on the headset talking to coaches Lane Kiffin in the booth and Steve Sarkisian on the sideline, along with Matt. We decided to go for the touchdown instead of spiking the ball to stop the clock. We chose to run a quarterback sneak, a play we ran every Friday in practice. With fellow soon-to-be Heisman Trophy winner Reggie Bush to his left, Matt tucked under center. Matt would be the first to admit that Notre Dame's defensive line was stacked right in front of him, and he even peeked back at Reggie as if to say, "What do you think?" Reggie gave him a nod that said,

"You got this," and Matt turned back under center. He took the snap and followed his center and fellow captain, Ryan Kalil, toward the goal line. Initially blocked, he spun to his left, and with an ever-so-slight nudge from Reggie, his six-foot-five frame found the end zone, sealing the victory in dramatic fashion.

No writer could have scripted a more compelling series of events for that game. It's the kind of game that, as a football coach, you live for. That matchup has been called "a game for the ages" and would have been a great day for college football whatever the outcome, though obviously we were happy seizing the win, 34–31, as well as holding on to our streak.

Yet while that final touchdown is perhaps the most famous play of that game, my favorite highlight is the moment when, on fourth and nine, Matt called the audible and our team reacted perfectly, as one. We had checked to "Red 82 Stay" countless times in practice, preparing for a situation precisely like fourth and nine. It was an instance of extraordinary poise, the best possible representation of all we had worked to create over the course of hundreds of competitive repetitions in practice. It was a moment that I hoped Coach Walsh would be proud of, a perfect example of the contingency planning he had shared with me back in San Francisco.

The poise and precision our guys showed that day was the strongest verification of our belief that "Practice Is Everything." Our practices were where we made ourselves into the team we needed to be. It was by practicing that we developed our ability to perform regardless of the circumstances.

Was there a downside to our open-practice policy? Were we giving up anything in return for a dynamic, competitive, and productive environment we created by keeping our practices open? Not much, in my opinion. Our opponents already had access to our game film, so we were not worried about giving anything away.

Open practices also gave us opportunities to connect with our fans. I remember as a young person waiting to get an autograph or to meet one of my heroes in person after a game. Now, being on the other side of that encounter, I always make an effort to live up to the obligation those memories represent. Whether they were coming from far away or right down the street, the kids who came to our practices were getting the opportunity to see what a realized dream looks like. And that sense of connection to the community around us was something we took very seriously. Believe it or not, many years earlier, Keyshawn Johnson, a Trojan and NFL wide receiver, was one of those grade-school kids who used to hang around practice at USC.

Like many teams, we would schedule visits for community groups, youth sports teams, local businesses, and other organizations. There was always something special about knowing we were open to anyone who cared enough about us to stop by.

Offering that experience wasn't why we started having open practices, but once we came to understand what a chance it gave us to share something special with our fans, the idea of not doing it became almost unthinkable.

The presence of fans also gave us an opportunity to teach the players about off-the-field behavior. The quarterbacks were surrounded by autograph seekers before they were even off the field, as were many other players. We all made a point of trying to make sure we didn't disappoint them. It was a great opportunity for our players to connect with the responsibility of being role models and to interact with their fans.

Obviously, football teams have secrets. I am as careful about guarding our playbooks and prospect evaluations as corporate executives are in guarding their portfolios or client lists, or as you are in guarding your Social Security and credit card numbers. And even though we had open practices, we did have certain restrictions on filming or photographing. We caught people trying to do it from distant buildings from time to time, and on the road we had to be on the lookout for that as well. Just because we were open didn't mean we were foolish. But that's all small stuff compared to the benefits we got from having a crowd on hand to watch us practice.

16

OUR RECRUITING PROMISE

At USC, we were very sensitive about making typical hard-sell promises to our recruits. So we promised them one thing: an extraordinary opportunity to compete for a position from the moment they arrived on our campus. In my nine years at USC we had freshmen starting at every position, including quarterback. As far as I know, no other team in college football has done that. I cannot overstate what an advantage it gave us. Our veteran players knew that if they did not compete to their fullest at all times there was nothing to keep a young guy from taking their place. And for the recruits, knowing they had the opportunity to compete from day one made them work harder, smarter, and with more ambition. We conveyed our expectation that every incoming player had the chance to start in his first year. That wasn't just a promise; we expected it.

The competitive opportunities proved to be an incredibly powerful recruiting tool. However, we didn't have this policy just to attract recruits. We discovered that by setting these high expectations and using supporting, consistent language, we could enable a freshman to contribute immediately.

When we recruited players, we always made a point of explaining that our goal was not to make them Heisman Trophy winners or All-Americans. We didn't promise trophies, titles, or even that they would start—much less play. As coaches, we would create opportunities for them to show their value and worth to the team and perhaps earn a starting position. What we did promise at USC, and will continue to do so at the Seahawks, is that all players, be they freshmen or rookies, seniors or veterans, would be given an equal opportunity to compete for a spot right away. That wasn't a sales pitch—it was the truth.

By being open-minded that first-year players could help us win, instead of thinking that they would get us beat, we felt we created an advantage at USC. Most personnel guys in the NFL think that playing rookies is the last thing a coach would want to do. But when I arrived at USC as the head coach and the man responsible for our personnel, I quickly altered my perspective on prospects.

In fact, we began to rely on freshman playing a significant role immediately. We discovered that their game experience contributed not only to early-season victories, but also provided depth and production late in the season. It's probably no coincidence that USC went undefeated in November for eight consecutive seasons.

There is probably no better example of someone contributing from the outset than former Trojan Reggie Bush. It's amazing that it took us so long to decide to offer Reggie a scholarship because his film was so unusual that we couldn't really tell what sort of player he would turn out to be. When I'm looking at prospects, the most important things I'm looking for are competitive will and love of the game. It was obvious Reggie had extraordinary talent, but it was his desire to separate from the crowd to be special that we questioned.

With Reggie, it was just so easy for him in high school that it was hard to tell. I must have watched his high school film thirty times, and time after time he was jogging into the end zone with no one else in the frame. I remember during one of our recruiting meetings I learned that his high school quarterback was Alex Smith, who would go to play at Utah and eventually be selected by the 49ers, as the first overall pick of the 2005 NFL draft. For all the times I studied those tapes before making a decision, I had never noticed Alex—I just couldn't take my eyes off Reggie. He was just so fast. Once we got him to USC, it only took a few minutes into the first practice to see that he was going to be a great contributor, but until we knew that, we could only hope that in addition to his extraordinary talent, he had that competitive drive. He did, of course—in a tremendous way, as he left USC with a Heisman Trophy and as an All-American, and this past season helped the New Orleans Saints become Super Bowl champions.

It's a common misconception that coaches dislike hitting the recruiting trail, traveling around the country, and driving from high school to high school. The truth? Some like it and some don't. Before I went back to college football, other coaches told me that recruiting was a burden. However, for me recruiting was just another way to compete. Once again the philosophy came through as we found ourselves immersed in just another competitive arena. We found ourselves in a "relentless pursuit of a competitive edge" in recruiting and it took us right back to our central theme of competition. This was not only a perfect extension of everything we were trying to do at USC, but also a great job by the recruiting coordinators I was able to work with, Ed Orgeron, Lane Kiffin, and Brennan, my oldest son. Our recruiting classes were at or near the top for eight straight seasons, and that is a credit to our entire coaching staff.

Recruiting was our chance to meet the players who would become the lifeblood of our program. It was as important as anything we did. As we would build our team each off-season, there was nothing more exciting than meeting the families and coaches of our prospects. USC offered a unique situation, as we were able to recruit some of the most talented athletes in America. What was even more exciting was that we felt that each freshman truly had a chance to play for us in the fall.

The recruiting process has accelerated and intensified in recent years, due in part to the Internet and the increased media attention paid to promising high school players. These developments—and the sometimes sensible, sometimes not-so-sensible rules that have been put in place to protect recruits or promote prospects—have altered the rhythm of the process and made it all more formal. The fundamentals of what we were looking for remained the same, and they always would, as skills and talent were just the beginning of the process, but surely not the end. They may have been enough to bring you into our selection process, but if that was all you had to offer, that process was going to be a short one. We needed something additional on top of that, something that would translate into an uncommonly competitive performer.

Every year at USC, we would recruit the most talented high school players in the country—kids with exceptional raw abilities, who were also being recruited by most other major football programs. You wouldn't really think that confidence would be a problem, but in fact, we found that this was a very important issue. I don't care how much of a star you had been in high school or how much raw talent you might have; coming to the USC football program was like getting dropped into the deep end of the pool. Virtually every member of the team possessed equal or greater talent, and certainly the older players had more experience. Not every recruit was equipped to handle this situation, so we looked for players who showed the kind of fortitude it took to compete at a college program already filled with topflight athletes.

This isn't just a football thing—it's a dynamic that leaders have to learn to manage in any organization that recruits the best to work alongside the best. Not only were we watching out for the younger players and nurturing their confidence, but we also needed to continually support and challenge the veterans. We knew we were walking a fine line in creating this competitive culture.

My favorite part of recruiting at USC was sitting in a player's living room, learning about his family and how he was raised. It was extremely important for me to meet our recruits' families, but even more important was that a recruit's family had a chance to meet our staff and me. After all, they would be sending their son to Los Angeles, sometimes far away from home in Florida, New Jersey, or Texas, with the trust that I would care for him as if he were my own child.

On National Signing Day, when we would add twenty or so top recruits to our program, we had a team meeting where we showed a highlight film of those incoming freshmen to our returning players. I reminded them that our staff had told those young players being featured on the big screen that they would be getting a fair shot from the moment they stepped on campus to compete for a starting position. It was a fun meeting, as the players suddenly became expert analysts, critiquing the incoming players who, more than likely, would be going after their spot. It was a blast to observe this meeting, as we were sure to remind the veterans that they had been told exactly the same thing when they had arrived on campus. It proved to our entire team that there was always an opportunity for every player to compete.

Our players knew that the only way to earn the right to be on the field was by competing for it, and they also knew that we would respond accordingly. When a recruit arrived as a freshman, we respected the effort he had put into his preparation to be there. We were far more wary of setting expectations too low than of setting them too high, and by placing great expectations on our student-athletes, our coaching staff had the belief they could field a championship team year after year.

17

MAKING IT FUN

I will be the first to admit that the coaching profession is demanding and the pressure is real. However, this is the job and the life we coaches have chosen, so how we deal with it is up to us. We can live the experience any way we choose. My choice is to take on the challenges and all that accompanies coaching and find the enjoyment and the fun whenever possible. It is my guess that most observers, even though they often see a grim expression on the faces of the coaches on the sidelines, would think that those same coaches have a great job and would give anything to have that opportunity. Well, I agree—I think coaching is a great job and I feel fortunate to be in such a position. To me the best thing in the world is to play the game, but when your playing days are over, the next best thing is to be right there coaching. I see the opportunity to coach as a blessing and it is my goal to enjoy it.

Anyone close to me knows I am always looking for the fun in everything I do, and I have always been that way. As a head coach, I feel the responsibility of making the working environment for the staff and the players an enjoyable one. The celebrations in a victorious locker room are the most fun of all. However, there are not enough games and victories to match the enormous amount of time we spend preparing for those winning moments, so we seize opportunities to have fun whenever we can find them. One example of seizing the moment happened in practice this past season on a rare rain-swept day in southern California.

It was "Competition Tuesday" and practice had ended with the offense and defense tied. We didn't have ties on Competition Tuesday—someone won and someone lost, period. Typically, what I did in a situation like that was just add one more play to the practice script and let our players settle the score on the field, but that day I felt like changing things up. It was pouring rain, somewhat uncommon in southern California, so instead of having one final play to determine that day's winner I decided to have Pat Ruel, our offensive line coach, and Jethro Franklin, our defensive line coach, go up against each other to determine who would prevail that day.

Our players created two lines, one with the offense and one with the defense, an either side of the largest puddle we could find. Whichever coach dove and slid the farthest through that puddle would earn the win for his side. As the players chanted back and forth, Pat and Jethro started to jaw as only O-line and D-line coaches can. Pat went first and slid about twenty yards. Jethro followed and, believe it or not, slid to the same exact spot! We couldn't end in a tie, so the coaches had to slide again. This time, Jethro edged out Pat by two feet. The defense went wild and as you might imagine, Pat was not very happy.

Our coaches at USC were very serious about teaching the game of football, but like that teacher you can remember who made class fun in high school, our coaches made sure our learning environment was fun too. They wanted to create a setting in their meeting rooms that the players looked forward to, and that was enormously critical to our success. We wanted the learning environment to al-

ways be alive and engaging, and we wanted our learners to arrive
each day anticipating what might happen next. We did things just
to keep it fresh. Part of our job as teachers is to entertain and surprise our students. Remember, the idea is to keep them fascinated
with what's going on, so they keep coming back, wondering what
will happen next.

Depending on who you are and what kind of organization you
are a part of, there are a million different ways to create moments to
uplift the atmosphere around your workplace. You will not be successful with every effort, and not all of your ideas will be equally
effective or appropriate. In our program, I've always had a penchant
for practical jokes and pranks, so that is one of the things we became
known for over the years at USC. It may have been just another
Monday-afternoon meeting, but you never knew what was going to
happen. Even after our guys learned that pranks were something
that was part of our culture, it was amazing how often we were able
to fool them. As the years went on, it actually became easier—which
was great for us, because there would always be those times when
we needed to deliver a dose of energy if we wanted to change the
tempo.

One of my favorites, the rooftop prank, got its start in Minnesota at the Vikings training camp in Mankato with the help of linebacker coach Monte Kiffin and a player named Keith Millard, who
played defensive tackle for the Vikings. Keith was a great player with
somewhat of a volatile personality, which made him a great cocon-
spirator in this case. We arranged for Monte to rib Keith in the
locker room before practice, and Keith responded by pretending to
go berserk—to the point where the rest of the team had to jump in
and separate the two of them and prevent what seemed like was
going to be a real fight. Later, when we got to the practice field, I
wondered aloud where the two of them were, and of course nobody

knew—until someone spotted them going at it on the roof of a nearby building, like a pair of six-foot-five gladiators! The two fought until they disappeared from sight for a second, and then over the edge comes what looks like Monte, with Keith standing behind him roaring like a madman. Of course, it was just a mannequin dressed up in coaching gear, but in the heat of the moment we had absolutely everybody fooled, until a moment later when Keith and Monte—alive and well—came running out onto the practice field.

The rooftop prank was enacted once again more recently on a Halloween night at USC. We wanted to do it with Reggie Bush, but he was hesitant to go up on the roof. Instead, we decided to try it with another running back, LenDale White. During practice I began to rip on LenDale for lack of effort among other things, and according to our plan he began to talk back. After what seemed like an eternity of back talk and generally disruptive behavior, LenDale blurted out, "I quit!" He threw his helmet to the ground and stormed off the field. Our players were in shock, but I made them get back to practice. At the end of practice I brought the team together and told them how proud I was of them for practicing well in spite of that distraction. All of a sudden I was interrupted by one gasp and then another. "Coach," someone shouted, pointing to a nearby rooftop, "Look, there's LenDale up there." Sure enough, there he was, shouting some obscenities, then disappearing from sight. The next thing you know, a dummy wearing LenDale's jersey came flying off the rooftop. About a quarter of the team thought LenDale had actually jumped. Many of the players fell to the ground in shock. Not everyone thought that this prank was such a good idea, but it would become part of the lore around USC.

Because we allowed opportunities for spontaneity, great moments just grew naturally out of the environment. In my last season at USC, "Lean on me" became an early-season motto for the team, although not through my own doing. It began during training camp as our upperclassmen got to know the newcomers. As in all training camps, the team spent an enormous amount of time together and got to know one another on a variety of levels. It turned out that one of our freshman linebackers could sing, and as soon as the boys found out, he was called out in one of our nightly team meetings. As they began to chant his name, pressuring him to perform, he obliged. As he stood in front of the room, a mere eighteen years old, he began to sing one of the best versions of the song "Lean on Me" you could imagine. After a moment or two, our players began to stand up, one by one, and interlock arms. They began to sway back and forth and sing along. In that moment during training camp, we had chosen our theme for the year.

As that training camp continued, the days got longer and the practices harder. The players, feeling the tension of being around the same faces for weeks on end, decided to stage a mock fight at the end of practice, as a way of turning the tables on the staff. As I jumped in the middle of it, preparing to restrain and discipline our squad, they all burst into laughter. I had been set up, but the following night I would be sure to get them back.

During our evening meeting an unfamiliar man entered. Following my introduction, he began his speech by telling the players that he was an NCAA official and had been summoned to USC to tell the players about a nasty shower fungus that was associated with bone damage. He was fairly convincing as he described the symptoms and dangers of the fungus. As the players began to look around nervously, wondering if they had already contracted the shower fungus, the man at the front of the room came clean, proclaiming, "You've been punked!" But that wasn't the best part—not by a long shot. The "official" then introduced himself—it was Bill Withers, the singer-songwriter who created "Lean on Me."

Bill called up that same freshman linebacker and sat down at the piano to intro "Lean on Me." The room quickly became a choir of players and coaches singing his famous piece. It was a great effort by Bill to come that night and we all have a memory that will last forever.

One of our greatest attractions over the years was our relationship with comedian Will Ferrell. Will was an undergraduate student at USC back in the day and a dedicated frat boy. He loves the Trojans and contributed in a big way by participating in numerous pranks over the years. Will's first prank came on his birthday back in 2003 as we were preparing for the Rose Bowl against Michigan. His friends called and asked if Will could come to practice and make an appearance and actually practice with the team. I said, "Sure, we would love to have him. Just make sure he arrives before we end practice." This was our first encounter with Will punking the team, and I did not know what to expect.

As luck would have it, he was running late, having trouble getting into his uniform. I had told the players in the morning meeting that some guy from a fraternity had called and asked if he could come out for the team, telling me he could help us beat Michigan. When I made the announcement, veteran players looked at me like I had lost my mind. I quickly passed it off by saying, "Whatever it takes, we need all the help we can get!" I left it at that, and hoped the surprise would be entertaining. As we dragged out our final drill of the day, a golf cart entered the practice field from the far end. I stopped practice and declared, "Here comes the new guy." Wearing number eighty-five in full game uniform, the new guy approached the team. The offensive squad was told to huddle up and call "I Right Action 2 X-Amigo R-Burst," a play-action pass calling for the split end to run a "go" route. Before anybody could figure out what was going on, we instructed the new guy to split out wide, get off the line of scrimmage, and "go long." I had a sudden rush of panic, thinking the right cornerback might knock Will's head off. I rushed over to tell Marcell Allmond to let Will run by him and not touch him. As luck would have it, Matt Leinart realized what was going on, and lofted a spiral to Will Ferrell plodding up the sideline. To his credit Will made the catch and stumbled into the end zone for the one and only touchdown reception of his career. And, needless to say, a star was born on the USC Trojan practice field. The players rushed over to Will, jumped on his back and had a great time. Fortunately, we went on to win the Rose Bowl, and I think Will took a good deal of the credit for inspiring the team.

This would be the first of many encounters with Will and the Trojans. He made a surprise appearance as "Ricky Bobby" from the film *Talladega Nights* in full race car regalia; we raced in a charity event called "Swim with Mike"; and he showed up to practice as the superhero "Captain Compete," saving a stuntman who fell off the filming scaffold, and even extinguishing another stuntman who was on fire on the practice field. Most recently, Will hosted an extraordinary fund-raiser at the NOKIA Theatre at L.A. Live, raising nearly a million dollars for A Better LA, my foundation. He truly has made great efforts to bring fun to the Trojans over the years and I couldn't be more appreciative.

There have been a number of priceless moments shared with the team and coaches, way too many to recount. The fact that USC is in the heart of Los Angeles and down the road from Hollywood afforded us many opportunities to connect with actors, entertainers, and notable sports figures on a fairly regular basis. I will always be grateful to all the wonderful people who contributed to make our experience at USC so special.

At the beginning of this chapter, I stated that the best fun for a football team is celebrating in a victorious locker room. The process of getting to that locker room is long and arduous. Whatever it takes to make the journey fun and engaging is worth it to me. Outsiders would be staggered by the effort we would make to keep the players guessing, never letting them in on what was coming next, just to enhance the impact of the upcoming event. No one had more fun than me, and I guess competing to pull off another prank on the players was a way of keeping me engaged and tuned in as well.

There is somewhat of a method to the madness behind the effort to make it fun and keep the team entertained. First, stirring up the environment we worked in is designed to keep it fresh and alive. We are teachers committed to our players learning at an extremely high level. That learning will directly affect how well prepared they are and how well they ultimately perform. A thriving learning environment has to increase the attention of our players. Second, there is an underlying message to convey to your team as you demonstrate confidence in them. When you allow them the opportunity to enjoy a change of tempo at the expense of a meeting or practice you are demonstrating that you believe in them. As I have said earlier, any way you can bolster the players' confidence and demonstrate your belief in them will make them stronger.

Over the years, our players have developed a unique ability to quickly transition between being serious and being lighthearted. They have developed the skill to do this because on any given day, we might change the tone and tempo of meetings or practice. Dealing with and practicing how you control your emotions, if done well, can become a valuable asset for an individual performer or a team. In football, the momentum swings in any game can cause a team to vacillate from one end of the spectrum to the other. To effectively handle major swings of emotion in a game is a skill that will allow a player to perform at his best. An example of the command of this skill was observed back in 2008 versus Ohio State.

Our 2008 matchup against the Buckeyes was about as hyped-up a contest as you get to see. Each team had played in two of the past four national championships, but we had not taken the field against each other in nearly twenty years. The energy at the Coliseum that day was wild. Going into the game, we were ranked number one and Ohio State number five, but the outcome was anyone's guess. Ohio State was coming into the Coliseum that day, and more than ninety-two thousand fans had made sure there wasn't an empty seat. Through-out that week, our players had to deal with the concept of a "big game" and the pressures that can be associated with that, but they handled it like it was any other game. We practiced well, stayed fo-cused, and prepared for the matchup. As we sat in the locker room minutes before the game, I recall looking over to the alums and boosters in the hallway and noticing them sweating bullets. I couldn't help but smile. They were so serious and so worried that it was almost painful, and none of them even had to play a snap!

Our players were loose and relaxed as if they were just going into another practice. With all that pressure on them, they were confi-dent, poised, and excited to play the game. Noticeably, they were playful and very comfortable even as game time drew near. Why? It wasn't because they took the moment for granted or because they felt for one second that victory was somehow assured. It was because no group could have worked harder to be ready for that moment or put more of themselves into the effort than our players.

Yet with everyone around them as tense as you could possibly imagine, I am proud to say that our players were just excited to play football. They knew they had put in all the work to prepare during the week and were looking forward to just cutting it loose on the field.

Our coaches could easily have spent those final moments telling their players how much was at stake, how important this win was for us, but they did not. What would have been the point? They knew the same thing our players did: The moment had arrived and they were ready to play ball.

The difference between our players' states of mind and that of the alums and boosters was not who was more serious—it was more a matter of us feeling loose and ready to play. Our guys knew that the only thing left to do was go out and perform like they had been prepared to do. And that is exactly what happened, as the Trojans dominated the game, winning 35–3.

18

PLAYING IN THE
ABSENCE OF FEAR

A head coach's primary objective is to orchestrate the overall mentality of his team. Great teams commonly display an air of confidence that separates them from others. They have earned the right to be confident through their hard work and success. The best teams utilize that confidence to share a feeling where they not only expect to win, they *know* they are going to win. That knowing is what allows a team to play in the absence of fear. That concept was the main objective and the ultimate focus throughout my nine years at USC and will also be now in Seattle.

When everything comes together for highly successful teams, they know they are going to win before they step out onto the field. This knowing is the most powerful state of mind for any team, and this is precisely what we set out to capture every season at USC. In my time as a coach I've learned that possibly the greatest detractor from high performance is fear: fear that you are not prepared, fear that you are in over your head, fear that you are not worthy, and ultimately, fear of failure. If you can eliminate that fear—not through arrogance or just wishing difficulties away, but through hard work and preparation—

you will put yourself in an incredibly powerful position to take on the challenges you face.

I am a firm believer in the idea that more often than not, people will live up to the expectations you set for them, and when it comes to our players, we set those expectations extremely high from their first day in the program—often even well beyond what the player himself thinks he can achieve—and we make sure they know it. High expectations are one of the most powerful tools we have. But we also understand that, if those expectations are unrealistic, inappropriate for the individual player in question, or so overwhelming and long term that players don't have the opportunity to enjoy smaller accomplishments along the way, then we are just setting our players up to fail.

Ideally, we want to create an atmosphere or a culture where our players can perform in the absence of fear. It is my job to orchestrate this "knowing we are going to win" mentality. Achieving that means finding ways to prove to players that they can rely on themselves and their teammates to perform at the highest level in the face of any challenge—even losing.

While the Win Forever philosophy sounds great when things are going well, what happens when things go wrong? How do you Win Forever given that everyone loses sometimes? The reality is that, no matter how well you practice, how fully you develop your philosophy, or how effectively you recruit, you will lose now and then. What separates those who have a true Win Forever outlook from those who don't is the ability to approach that challenge of losing with the same competitive spirit with which they approach everything else. When I say that "everything counts" or that every challenge in life is a chance to compete, I mean it. I don't mean "everything except losing." Personally, I hate to lose more than almost anything. What I hate even more is learning the hard way. I want that for the other guy. But in reality we can learn tremendously from our losses and our mistakes, though that is tough to admit.

Those setbacks, challenges, and hardships have been learning experiences, and I have learned to respect and appreciate them. In their own way, what they have taught me was as much a part of our Rose Bowl victories and national championships at USC as anything else I have picked up along the way.

In fact, it was in our most difficult moments at USC that I leaned on the Win Forever approach the most. We have had our share of disappointments, but few more dramatic than at the end of the 2005 season, when we faced the University of Texas in the BCS national championship game. We were twenty-six seconds away from winning an unprecedented third straight national title.

The Longhorns' quarterback, Vince Young, had delivered a superhuman effort all night, and we knew that he was sure to save his best for last. The game had gone back and forth all night. We had our offense, led by Matt Leinart, Reggie Bush, Steve Smith, Dwayne Jarrett, and LenDale White, performing at a high level—they even set a Rose Bowl record with 574 total yards of offense. But Texas also had a high-powered machine and kept the score close throughout the game.

Up 38–33 with 4:03 remaining, we needed a couple first downs to clinch a victory. We had practiced this situation numerous times and were confident that we could operate our "four-minute offense" and win the game. After all, moments like this were what we were all about as a team. After a short run by LenDale and a completion from Matt to Dwayne, we had one of the two necessary first downs to clinch the BCS championship. On first down we gave the ball back to LenDale for a three-yard gain, which got us to midfield. After an incompletion and another short run by LenDale, we were faced with fourth and two.

We were confident with our play call for this fourth and two situation, "27 Power Quad." LenDale had run it all season long with near-perfect success. He took the handoff and as he was forced to cut back, a Texas defensive lineman made a great play to take away his running lane. We were stopped inches short of the first down marker, giving the ball back to Texas.

As Young and his offense jogged onto the field with 2:13 left in the game, down 38–33, I knew our defense would have to make a play, as Young was performing in the proverbial "zone," with no sign of slowing down. He started by completing a pass for minus two yards, followed by an incompletion on second down. On third and twelve from the Texas forty-two-yard line, he completed a pass to Quan Cosby for seven yards, short of a first down. However, we were called for a facemask penalty, keeping the Longhorns drive alive.

Young completed a pass to Brian Carter for nine yards, ran for seven, and completed another pass for seventeen yards, moving his team to our thirteen-yard line with the clock winding down. We were calling all sorts of defenses as we pressured two linebackers on one snap, played coverage on the next, and brought a corner blitz on another, but Young kept at it. On first down, he threw an incomplete pass. On second, he ran for five yards, and on third and five from our eight-yard line he threw another incompletion out of the end zone to stop the clock. And there we were, fourth and five with only twenty-six seconds remaining.

The 93,986 fans were standing up—half screaming and half holding their breath. It was as magnificent a setting as any competitor could ask to be a part of. We decided to bring our two inside linebackers on a blitz and play man coverage. As Young dropped back, he went through his progression and stepped up in the pocket, avoiding our pressure. He took off to his right and we had no chance to catch him as he raced to the end zone for the game-winning touchdown.

That superhuman effort, which totaled 267 yards passing, plus 200 yards rushing on nineteen carries, for a total of 467 yards by one player, was a Rose Bowl record. As a result, Vince Young earned the game's MVP award.

As I entered the locker room following the game, I was racing to think of what I would tell the players. We had just had our thirty-four-game winning streak snapped and had fallen short of a third straight national championship. I decided to tell the truth:

> Men, we came within nineteen seconds of winning a third consecutive national title—nineteen seconds! To put in all of the work we put in, there is no way that nineteen seconds can define us as winners or losers. We've always said that for someone to beat us we either have to turn it over a number of times and give the game away or they have to play out of their minds, and tonight, number ten had one of the greatest single game performances in the history of college football, and still, we were only nineteen seconds away from winning! Give Texas all the credit in the world, but you're still champions. Nineteen seconds will never define you.

While I did not want to take anything away from Texas, as they were the superior team that night, I wanted our players to still feel like champions. It had been a historic season and one that our entire program should have been proud of. We were not going to let nineteen seconds define us. Because of the character of our players, and because they knew from experience that it is possible to play to your full potential and still not walk away with the win, we would not let that one loss define us.

Certainly we had other tough losses at USC. What is truly remarkable is how our players and coaches responded in every situation. By returning to the truth of who we were and by looking forward to the challenge of our next opponent, we were able to be incredibly resilient, in spite of any adversity. We never dragged the past along with us, because the past is not a place where we can compete. I think it is in part because we refused to do that in victory that we were so successful in moving on from a defeat. Instead, we focused on recapturing the essence of who we knew ourselves to be and on controlling what was directly in front of us, and then hit the practice field with the intention of getting better the very next day. We never allowed the disappointment of losing to diminish the attitude and energy we needed to bring every day.

When you have gotten to a place where you are as ready to embrace the learning opportunities given to you by the games you lose as to embrace the ones given to you by the games you win, then you are ready for all potential outcomes. That state of mind, when you are truly competing for the sake of performance alone, is when you are performing in the absence of fear, and I promise you that an organization that can get to that mind-set will succeed—will win—not just for a game or a season but from that moment onward.

19

SETTING A VISION AND SEEING IT

Growing up outside San Francisco, I was a casual fan of the Grateful Dead. I remember hearing an interview with the late, great guitar player and leader of the band, Jerry Garcia.

I can't remember exactly what question the interviewer asked him, but it was something along the lines of "How do you feel about being possibly the greatest rock-and-roll band of all time?" A classic softball question, but rather than responding with the usual fluff, Jerry said something I'll never forget. "No, man," he answered, ever so relaxed. "That's not how we think of ourselves at all. We don't want to be the best ones doing something—we want to be the only ones doing it."

That cool reply stuck in my head. And as I thought about it over the years, I came to realize what an important concept Garcia was onto. The best performers, whether athletes, entertainers, or anybody else trying to do anything well, are the ones who aren't trying to win by playing someone else's game. Each person is made up of a unique combination of strengths, weaknesses, abilities, and talents, and any one of us can only truly maximize our potential in the context of that individual makeup. That's why it doesn't make sense to think about competition in the context of any one opponent: If you are really in a Win Forever mind-set, the only comparison that matters is yourself. Your goal should be to maximize your potential and your performance as a permanent way of being, rather than just thinking in terms of individual victories.

Furthermore, one of the most important facets of the Win Forever approach is to help people see what they can become and then to support them. We want to help our players, both at USC and now in Seattle, make the connection with their potential until it becomes real for them. It's not so much about getting to that goal in a certain amount of time as it is about the process of working to get there. Once that confidence takes hold, you can see things start to happen. As a coach working to build confidence, you have to convince your players that not only do they have the power to control their performance, but they're the *only* ones who do. Other people can factor into their success, either by helping them realize their goals or by motivating them to get there, but it's the individual himself who ultimately is the only one who has the power to develop his fullest potential.

Getting that across to players is a constant occupation. You have to continually encourage people to the point where they feel empowered to call the shots that will position them to become the best they can be. It's not any one specific thing but rather an ongoing process of showing them what they're capable of.

Personally, I have learned that if you create a vision for yourself and stick with it, you can make amazing things happen in your life. My experience is that once you have done the work to create the clear vision, it is the discipline and effort to maintain the vision that can make it all come true. The two go hand in hand. The moment you've created that vision, you're on your way, but it's the diligence with which you stick to that vision that allows you to get there.

There are so many examples of the power of visioning. That power of creating a vision is so great that it can actually work for you as well as against you.

I clearly remember one day when I was visiting Watts, in Los Angeles. I asked a young man what his vision was for his life. His matter-of-fact response was "I'm either going to jail or I'm gonna die." Shocking as that was, the odds were that he was probably right, and they were increased by the fact that he was already laying out that path in his own mind. If there was ever a clear example of a negative affirmation, that was it. I could only respond by saying, "You're probably right. As long as that's the vision you hold for your life, that's likely what you're gonna get."

The power of one's vision and affirmations is incredibly strong. I have always believed that what you expect is usually what you get. You draw it to you. A great example of that was our 2004–2005 USC football team.

USC was playing the Oklahoma Sooners in Miami for the national championship. It was the night before the game, and I was searching for the right words to say.

It's not very often that I find myself at a loss for words when it comes to talking to the team the night before a game. After a while in this profession, you develop an instinct for what a team needs to hear at a given moment. But on the night of January 3, 2005, as I was preparing to address our USC Trojans on the eve of the national championship game, I was stumped. I just couldn't find a topic that felt big enough to fully convey everything I felt about this incredible group of people and what they had already achieved. I wanted to tell them how excited and confident I felt about going into the next day's game with the whole country watching. I didn't just want to remind them how much I believed in them—how certain I was that we were going to win. What I wanted—what I needed—was to make them feel the absolute truth of *why* I believed in them so deeply at that moment, of *why* the next day's outcome felt so sure to me. But the words kept eluding me. And the clock kept ticking.

We'd had an extraordinary lead-up to this national championship game. Both teams had a perfect year—something only one of us would still be able to say the following night. This was just one of the many reasons why the buildup had been so huge in the weeks leading up to the game. The media coverage had really gone overboard. The press was having a field day, with many predicting that the matchup could well turn out to be the biggest college game in history. The scrutiny and pressure were intense, but our guys had survived it with classic Trojan poise and style. We were in great shape, mentally and physically, going into the game. We had been through a month of preparation that had gone almost perfectly, and we were ready. The trip from Los Angeles to Florida, the stay at the hotel in Miami, everything had gone just as we had envisioned it. No one was getting distracted or into any trouble. Everyone was sticking to the script.

As a team, we couldn't have been closer. There were seniors on the team who had been freshmen when I arrived at USC, so in a sense we had all grown up together. The moment we were walking into was really the culmination of the ideas we had conceived and the program we had worked so hard to build. It felt as if every step of the way, everything had gone exactly as planned.

That feeling reminded me of a concept my friend Michael Murphy had introduced me to years earlier, something the researcher W. G. Roll called the "long body." Roll studied the way that group intentions manifested within Iroquois tribes. While his research falls into the realm of parapsychology, the concept really resonated with what we were experiencing at USC. When in a focused state similar to what Maslow calls "peak performance," individuals within the groups Roll studied seemed to develop a single consciousness, acting with one will. As Roll described it, "The Tribe is likened to a body connected where, once connected, it operates as a single entity functioning, sensing, and feeling as one. A Tribal-Mind-Body where members share a Tribal nature, a Communal nature, that they instinctively own, a Mental connection, a Knowing, a Long Body." When a team can get into that kind of state, the resulting group exhilaration and sense of invincibility allows them to see and reach potential they never would have dreamed of as individuals. It is as if the team shared one heartbeat.

I have traditionally used the night before a game as an opportunity to have a big meeting that sets the tone for our attitude and approach the next day. Still at a loss for an inspirational topic, I certainly wasn't about to pass on that night in Miami. It was ironic, really. After four years of work and dedication focused on a single vision, we were standing at the precipice of the biggest opportunity that you could ever have in college football—four years and thousands of hours of preparation to go from dream to reality, and fifteen minutes before our meeting I still didn't know what I was going to say to our guys.

Finally, it dawned on me that the reason I was struggling so much was that I just couldn't think of a more inspiring example to put in front of our guys than to tell them the truth about what we had accomplished. There was literally nothing I could say to them that would be more effective than simply reminding them how we had gotten to where we sat that night. Once I realized that, it was easy. Over time, they had all joined in and made a commitment by saying, "I'm in," which meant they had accepted the vision and philosophy of our program. By doing so, they had allowed us to push them to their limits, and here we were, the night before the national championship game, together one final time.

Every person in that room that night was there because he had made a commitment, practice by practice, game by game, to be a part of this program. Together they had committed to the vision to "do things better than they have ever been done before." As I entered the team meeting room, I knew I was looking at much more than just a soon-to-be-championship football team. I couldn't wait to tell them what we had accomplished, that they were living proof that you can create whatever you envision as long as you are willing to always compete and stay on course with your objective.

With total commitment and hard work, we had done just that. Now all we had to do was go play the game. This may have sounded overly confident or arrogant, but it wasn't even hard to say. We just knew it on the inside. What excited me the most was the realization that our players would be able to draw from this example long after the 2005 Orange Bowl.

The game turned out to be a wonderful celebration of a championship season. We had done something I had always dreamed of, winning every game and totally maximizing the potential of a season and a team. A philosophy had been shared by a group of young men and coaches and had resulted in a wonderful achievement on the field as we won 55–19. More important, the lessons learned both on and off the field would stay with us for a lifetime.

The philosophy we lived by had given us the guidelines and structure to create a championship program. The foundations for establishing a winning formula were in place. We had set a vision and stated an affirmation. Now the real challenge was on: Could we do it again? . . . and again? . . . and again?

20

WINNING FOREVER
ON AND OFF THE FIELD

The experience at USC carried far beyond the playing field. Working in our nearby communities allowed us the opportunity to reach out on numerous occasions to people from our surrounding neighborhoods. I will forever be grateful for all the relationships and the lives we touched late at night on the streets of LA. But in addition to our activities on the fields of USC and the work in the surrounding communities, there was another world of experiences we would encounter that no one could have predicted.

The principles of Win Forever, which remind us to compete and always strive to do our best, at times took on an entirely new meaning. We found ourselves as team members, challenged to not only endure some of life's most gripping tests, but also to respond and support in ways we never could have imagined. Principles so basic to our football team helped us hang together, and our ability to never stop competing on the field would prove instrumental off the field as well. We learned that being supportive would be crucial, as off-the-field challenges continued to come our way. And finally, our always enduring will to be positive and to hold on to the belief that something good was just about to happen, no matter how dire the circumstances, would truly prove to be worthwhile. We were continually inspired as a team by the strength and courage demonstrated by those individuals and families caught in the middle of the tragedies that everyday life sometimes brings. Our team at USC has shown this strength of character time and again.

On September 28, 2009, we were 3-1, and preparing for a big Pac-10 matchup against the University of California, Berkeley, when an assistant strength coach came rushing to my office. There had been an accident in the weight room, he told me, and Stafon Johnson was being rushed to the emergency room. He had been on the bench press when a bar loaded with 275 pounds slipped out of his hands and fell directly on his throat.

Bleeding from his mouth and nose, barely able to breathe, Stafon was rushed to the California Hospital Medical Center. During emergency surgery lasting for more than seven hours, doctors were miraculously able to repair a crushed larynx, damaged throat, and critically injured airway. After several more surgeries and weeks of recovery, the doctors credited his overall athleticism, fitness, and mental fortitude for his survival and said they expected him to make a full recovery.

Clearly, our first priority was Stafon's recovery and for a while, it wasn't clear whether or not he would be able to speak again. At the same time, his injury was a major blow to our team and our season. An extremely talented player, Stafon was also our emotional leader. In his absence, we were missing not only his skills but also his positive influence on the rest of the team.

When we arrived at Memorial Stadium that weekend, our players were prepared to play but naturally had Stafon's health weighing on their minds. That night, in our team meeting, the coaches and I talked to the team about playing with the passion Stafon had, the poise he embodied, and the strength he possessed. My hope was that, if we couldn't have him playing with us, at least we'd have the example of his courage to push the team to play their best, and we did. That Saturday night, our players kept the motto "Lean on Me" going, and defeated Cal 30–3.

Our 2009 season was an uncharacteristic one for us, as we endured four losses, all within our conference, to Washington, Oregon, Stanford, and Arizona. Each one of those losses tore me apart. As coaches get older, the losses begin to outweigh the victories, but there was something that helped me keep my perspective: meeting and getting to know a very special young man named Jake Olson.

Mark Jackson, USC senior associate athletic director for football, met the Olson family prior to our game at Notre Dame. They had wanted to bring their twelve-year-old son, Jake, to South Bend to watch the Trojans, his favorite team. We love our young fans, but this was no ordinary fan. Jake was about to undergo surgery that would take his vision away from him.

Jake had been diagnosed at the age of one with a condition known as retinoblastoma, or cancerous tumors, in both eyes. Doctors had been forced to remove his left eye when he was a baby, but with chemotherapy and radiation, they had been able to save his right eye. That right eye had shown Jake his world. It had shown him his parents, Cindy and Brian, his twin sister, Emma, and eventually USC football. Jake was an outgoing kid and he came right up to me at practice. He knew our players inside and out and had a special fondness for our center, a position he played on his flag football team.

The ultimate competitor, Jake had beaten cancer eight times, but the ninth time, that September, the disease got the best of him. Doctors told him that they would have to remove his right eye, leaving him blind. It was a heartbreaking situation, but at least we were able to give him one of the things he wanted most—to see USC play Notre Dame in person.

We tried to make Jake's experience memorable by including him in our Friday walk-through, pregame activities, locker-room frivolity, and my postgame press conference. He had a blast in South Bend, taking in the game day experience with his family and enjoying the victory with our players.

The following weekend, Jake was our guest again, this time at the Los Angeles Memorial Coliseum. From the team bus to the postgame locker-room celebration, Jake was involved in everything. After the game, we spoke and he told me how much fun it had been to ride with the guys on the bus, participate in the Trojan walk, and hear the team chant his name in the locker room after our 42–36 win over Oregon State.

We endured some tough losses in the next few weeks, but as Jake was preparing for surgery, he was our inspiration. He was doing everything he could with his last few weeks of vision, and doing it with a sense of competitiveness and dignity that would have been extraordinary for anyone, much less a twelve-year-old.

The night before the surgery he came to practice and hung out with our guys. When someone asked him if he was scared, Jake replied that it wasn't so much blindness he was frightened of as it was the prospect of not making the most of those last few hours and minutes of sight. Hearing that gave us all a new perspective. Here was a twelve-year-old kid, the personification of courage, on the verge of losing his vision, and here we were, grown men feeling sorry for ourselves after losing a few games.

Six days after surgery Jake showed up at Heritage Hall, making good on a promise to our players. When he walked in the door on Monday afternoon, our team was jacked to see him in spite of the fact that we had been dealt a tough loss only two days earlier. In the face of his example, there was no room for pessimism or negativity. He may have been a boy among men, but it was we who leaned on him. The presence of someone as strong as he was, as confident as he seemed, and as impressive as he sounded was something we all needed.

Jake was on the sideline for our next game against UCLA, a victory, and in the locker room afterward. As we sang our fight song and shared high fives all around, I couldn't help but watch Jake and just be blown away by his competitive nature. While it could be said that cancer beat Jake on the ninth attempt, I think all of us at USC would disagree. Jake still won, just in a different sort of way.

Another member of the Trojan family who provided leadership and inspiration even in tragedy was placekicker Mario Danelo. One of the most lovable players in the history of our program, he lived by the motto "Living the Dream," and whether on the practice field or with his incredible family, he competed to do just that.

In 2003, Mario walked on to our program, and by 2005 he was our placekicker, on full scholarship. Naming Mario our starter was easy, as he was different from most kickers. A high school all-conference linebacker, he approached the position with a linebacker's mentality. His intense approach and focus allowed him to perform in the absence of fear. There was also a family legacy I noticed with Mario. Before every game, as he warmed up with the other specialists, I would observe his demeanor and think back to my days in the NFL when his father, Joe, was our kicker in Buffalo. Joe was also a tough competitor who carried himself in a joyful manner. When his son expressed an interest in becoming a Trojan, we were thrilled to give him an opportunity.

On January 6, 2007, five days after our 32–18 Rose Bowl victory over Michigan, Mario died in a tragic accident when he fell from a 120-foot cliff near his home in San Pedro, California. The grieving process was difficult for our team, as many of the players had never experienced the loss of someone close to them. Mario's funeral at

Mary Star of the Sea Catholic Church aided the process and was something we'll always remember. The church was filled to capacity with family and loving friends, and the surrounding streets were lined with neighbors, fans, and supporters.

I was asked to speak at his service, a challenging and emotional task. As I prepared my speech, I could only think about Mario and how much he appreciated those around him, how he was a natural leader, and how he never backed off his desire to keep "Living the Dream." As I approached the podium that Friday morning, I kept remembering how each Saturday afternoon Mario would soak in the wonder of living his dream as the USC Trojans' starting placekicker.

Mario was a wonderful young man and a real team player. His loss was heartbreaking to his family and our team. So on this very sad morning, I wanted to bring him back into the room one last time. We needed to feel his presence, and the best way I knew to do that was to involve every person in the congregation. I asked every-one in the crowd to stand up. I reminded them how much Mario loved making field goals for the Trojans and how he enjoyed the crowd's reaction afterward. Speaking from my heart, I said, "Let's be sure Mario can hear us. Let's be sure he can feel us one more time, just like it is every Saturday in the Coliseum. And while he won't be there with us next season to get the cheers he deserves, let's be sure to let him hear us one more time. Let's give Mario the ova-tion he deserves."

As the cheers rang out for Mario, I was overcome with emotion and heartache. The crowd got louder and louder, more and more passionate, and I too was caught up in the moment as the gathering gave Mario one last cheer.

We opened the very next season hosting the University of Idaho at the Coliseum. After we forced them to punt on their first possession of the game, John David Booty led our offense on a ten-play, eighty-yard drive that resulted in a Stafon Johnson four-yard score. Our special teams unit ran onto the field for the extra point attempt with one player obviously missing, the placekicker. The crowd immediately sensed the oversight, but we had a plan and soon enough the crowd understood what we were doing. The Trojan faithful rose to their feet to honor Mario one last time. I wish I could take credit for the idea to pay special tribute to Mario, but it actually came from Mario's teammates, who would keep his memory and his dream alive throughout the coming season and beyond. It was the single most moving moment of my time at USC.

As a team we so often talk about being like a family, and with the sacrifices coaches and players make, we forgo important times with our own families. An example that was close to home for me was with my youngest son, Nate. Because we played on Saturdays, our Friday nights were spent at a team hotel, either on the road or in downtown Los Angeles. On Fridays we had an unbreakable ritual: from the practice field to Heritage Hall for a pep rally with the band, to the bus that was going to take us to the hotel where we'd stay until taking the field the next day. Those nights were always filled with meetings and preparations and it was vitally important that we kept the same routine. My family understood the day-to-day obligations of coaching a football team, and often had to do things without me. If I have any regrets, they are not being able to attend many of my children's school functions or sporting events.

One Friday night, during my youngest son Nate's senior football season, I decided that I had to find a way to attend his play-off game. Breaking a long-standing tradition, I switched the format of our normal Friday-night meeting so that I could watch Nate play quarterback for the first time, as he took over for the injured starter. As the team listened to the change in schedule they automatically expected to jump on our team bus and come along. Were it not for NCAA regulations, I might have considered it. After all, it wasn't unusual for us to pull a surprise field trip to go bowling or attend a professional beach volleyball tournament. I can't say what a thrill it was for me to see Nate's team win their game, and as luck would have it, another one the following week during our bye.

When I arrived at USC, I had a newly developed philosophy for how to build a program that I hoped would Win Forever. It was drawn from my experiences and based on things I had learned in my previous twenty-two years as a coach. But I never thought I would learn as much as I did during my time at USC, on and off the field. There was more love and heartfelt exchanges than I ever could have imagined. From celebrating victories to weathering hardships, the warmth and the love that were shared will never be forgotten.

PART FOUR

WIN FOREVER BEYOND THE FIELD

21

NOT JUST FOOTBALL

You might think that football is merely a game and the lessons that apply to playing this game might not have much to do with the "real" world. What does a touchdown have to do with life off the football field? My answer: a lot. Maybe not the touchdown itself, but what it takes to make a touchdown—all the hard work, all the practice, and the dedication to perform at your best—is as valuable off the field as on.

I am very lucky that I have a job I love doing and am so passionate about, but I also realize that I am still part of a larger world. How I interact with that world—with my family and my community—is very important to me. I want to be someone who competes just as hard to be a best friend, loving husband, caring parent, and active community member as I do to be an excellent football coach.

About seven years ago, in 2003, I was driving into work along the side streets of south Los Angeles and I heard on the radio that another young kid had been slain in gang-related violence, bringing the total to eleven homicides for the week. I work with young men, some of whom easily could have fallen into the cycle of gangs, were it not for their talent, or, more important, support from their families, teachers, and coaches. So news of that kind struck close to home for me. That day, for whatever reason, it hit me especially hard, and I decided to call my good friend Lou Tice.

Lou is the founder of the Pacific Institute, a self-empowering educational program. He and I had been talking for a while about finding a way to make a major impact in the community. The timing then felt as right to him as it did to me. We started mapping out an organization that would eventually be known as A Better LA.

Our mission would be to save the lives of young children and reduce gang-related violence in Los Angeles. We would do it through community building, youth empowerment, and professionally trained prevention and intervention workers.

I have been overwhelmed by the dedicated work of these incredible heroes who have affected me with their life stories. My closest friend from the neighborhood, Bo Taylor, was a strong, humble, and caring father and leader on the streets of LA. Bo taught me about the work that needed to be done and introduced me to people across the city in hopes of reaching communities in need. The unsung heroes are intervention and community outreach workers, and they live deep in my heart for their courage, leadership, and willingness to protect the communities they love. Bo passed away in 2008 but through his inspiration, the communities have accomplished extraordinary feats, and with continued support from the mayor, law enforcement, and local neighborhoods, the work continues. Strong leadership continues to prevail from within the community thanks to the dedicated work of outreach workers like Aquil Basheer, Cornell Ward, Gary Robinson, Reynaldo Reaser, and so many others. A model for sustainable change has been created and we are reaching out to more neighborhoods to increase the impact.

Seven years since our inception, gang violence is still an issue, but the city of Los Angeles has seen an unprecedented decline in homicides and aggravated assaults, particularly in the areas where A Better LA has concentrated its efforts. The cooperation of local communities, government, law enforcement, and the private sector has been exceptional. And while I love coaching football and watching my team win, I have to admit that the work of A Better LA and the influence it has had on these communities is, in the long run, more important. It has also been very gratifying to witness my daughter, Jaime, help carry out the vision of A Better LA with peace rallies, fund-raising efforts, and annual community events. I am proud not only of the work she does, but of how much of her heart and soul she puts into it.

The power of affirmations is incredibly strong. Because I have always believed that what you expect is usually what you get, what you focus on is what you draw to yourself. We have the power to create our own reality and through a vision of hope, that concept is constantly at work for all of us. Our plan at A Better LA is to inspire that in one person at a time. Living and working in the greater Los Angeles area, as well as representing USC in general, has provided me countless opportunities to reach out to organizations, schools, and businesses. I am often asked to speak about the success of our football team and how our philosophy might apply to an individual or group.

One such person is Andy Bark, who has become a good friend. I was introduced to Andy about the time I accepted the job at USC. Back in the late 1980s, he had founded a company called Student Sports, a leading digital media company revolving around high school athletics, and had operated camps and clinics with corporate giants such as Nike and EA Sports. Andy had his finger on the pulse of thousands of high school athletes, but more important, he had a great understanding of the landscape of college football—which, after all, was what every high school football player had his eyes on.

A ball boy for USC and UCLA during the John McKay and Dick Vermeil eras and a wide receiver at Cal in the early 1980s, Andy clearly understood the development necessary for an athlete to succeed in college.

After talking about the history at USC and college football in general, I asked Andy if he would be interested in hearing my philosophy, because I thought it might be helpful to him and his company. After more than two hours of talking, I learned that Andy had sold his company in 2001 and had been unhappily watching it slow down in his absence. I could relate to his frustration, and we spent quite a while talking about the situation.

A week later, Andy called me with exciting news. He had decided to not only buy his company back but also reorganize its structure and start an athletic training business. Based on our conversations, he also decided to formulate a philosophy based on Win Forever principles and to create a vision for the new era of Student Sports.

By creating his own version of the Win Forever philosophy, Andy didn't just revitalize his organization; in 2008 he sold it to ESPN, which renamed the company ESPN RISE. Furthermore, his other training company, SPARQ, was bought by Nike in 2009.

Another lesson depicting how broadly the ideas that have been developed for coaching football could be applied elsewhere came when I was invited to speak to senior U.S. military leaders. The occasion was the Small Unit Excellence Conference, a first-of-its-kind seminar in Alexandria, Virginia, in April 2009, and I was privileged to join a diverse group of participants ranging from orchestra conductors to psychologists. The participants were looking at ways to apply the insights of our professional expertise to performance in the military. Our goal was to help set a foundation for revolutionary shifts in the actions and attitudes of the country's small-unit armed forces, such as the Navy SEALs, the Green Berets, and the Army Rangers.

The three-day event was cosponsored by the U.S. Department of Homeland Security and attracted some of the military's highest-ranking officers. They were seeking to answer a single fundamental question: How can the U.S. military improve and maintain consistent success?

Four-star general James Mattis, who commands the U.S. Joint Forces Command, was the keynote speaker and opened the conference. He set the tone for the days to follow by challenging the group to forgo conventional wisdom and think outside the box. There was a lot of energy in the room, and I had the feeling that this was a chance to contribute in a meaningful way to the performance of our servicemen and servicewomen. I was proud to be a part of something that stirred my sense of patriotism. It was the first time in my life I had felt this close to that calling, and I wanted to come through and help if I could.

I was assigned to a twenty-two-person breakout group, and we spent twelve hours each day going through a variety of workshops. My fellow participants were incredibly impressive, and I was so enthralled with what each speaker had to say that the time flew by. The group included top-ranking military officers and some of America's brightest academics, and I not only learned different philosophies and outlooks from them but almost had to chuckle at the thought that my experience as a football coach somehow qualified me to be a part of something like this. Yet at the same time I felt very comfortable as part of that team, and I realized once again that when it comes to leadership and performance, the basic principles are almost universal.

As the conference continued, I saw that what we had done at USC and what we were working to accomplish in the inner city of Los Angeles had really broad applications to teams of all kinds. In both football and our nonprofit work, as in the military, the objective is similar: Each team member must maximize his or her potential to perform effectively, with the success of the team depending not only on a single star performance but on everyone working together at their highest possible level. The major difference, of course, is that if we throw four interceptions and lose a game, life goes on. In the military, in places such as Iraq and Afghanistan, if someone doesn't do his or her job, lives are lost.

In our breakout groups we were asked to make recommendations to the conference for enhancing the performance of small-unit forces. My group asked me to kick off our segment by presenting the Win Forever approach as an overall vision for directing all small-unit activities throughout the armed forces.

From the beginning of the conference, it was evident that no single overriding philosophy yet existed, nor was there a common language to connect the individual units across the armed forces. Common themes, consistent language, and an all-encompassing vision could make it possible not only to elevate performance but also to foster a shared camaraderie among the military's many different groups. Win Forever, with its clear philosophy and terminology, we realized, could be a very effective vehicle for bringing the military groups together.

I have to say that I was a little nervous about addressing an audience of generals and admirals, but the presentation was extremely important to me.

It started in much the same way that our spring football meetings do, with my asking the entire audience to stand up and change seats. I was used to pulling this trick with twenty-year-olds in shorts and

T-shirts, so it was fun to see well-established professionals stand up, gather their papers, and unplug their laptops to move from one row to another. Not everyone appreciated it, but I had a point to make, and getting it across successfully started with getting the audience members out of their comfort zone.

I then asked the crowd how many of them had a philosophy. As you might assume, many of them raised their hands. Then I asked of those people who had just raised their hands, "How many of you could stand up right now and share your philosophy with us in twenty-five words or less?" As always, the hands dropped quickly around the room—including one hand I would have expected to remain in the air, the one belonging to conference director and decorated major general Dr. Robert Scales.

In addition to having commanded combat units in the Vietnam and Korean wars and earning the Silver Star, among many other honors, Major General Scales is widely regarded as one of our foremost experts on military training and education. He also helped design the army's training doctrine and has authored several books. Furthermore, Major General Scales's last posting was as commandant of the U.S. Army War College. You will now recognize him as an expert analyst who regularly appears on television.

When his hand dropped, I remember seeing a few nervous faces around him, clearly wondering how someone with his rank and prestige might react to getting singled out. But he didn't show a hint of embarrassment or discomfort. He just had this thoughtful, surprised smile on his face as he said, "You got me, Coach!" You could see that his mind was racing with the implications of the exercise.

Major General Scales is living proof that successful leaders can achieve extraordinary things without necessarily ever having asked themselves what exactly their philosophy is. He is one of many such high performers whom I have met over the years. Once the question was put in front of him, he recognized that by having a philosophy he could articulate, he could be even more effective. As a leader in a very unique field, he'll do that in his way and in a manner that is appropriate for his needs and goals. I am grateful to him for allowing me to participate in the conference and for helping me understand just how universal the basic principles of leadership, competition, and self-knowledge really are.

22

YOU CAN WIN FOREVER

All the things I have talked about in this book ultimately are just different expressions of the simple, basic life goal of being able to know yourself and define your philosophy in a way that is true to who you are. That's it. There are probably as many different ways to say that as there are people, but however it makes sense to you, I believe that is what it all comes down to. It is what we work toward in a football program and what I work toward as a person every day.

We all have setbacks and we all get derailed sometimes. In sports, your team loses a game. In business, CEOs miss projections for the year. In the military, a battle doesn't unfold as the general expected. What gets us back on track after such events is the clarity of our vision. If the goals, strategies, and techniques you have laid out for yourself are really true to your core self, you will always be able to get back to them. You will always *want* to get back to them.

You will make competing to stay on course with your vision the way you live your life every day. It takes discipline, and that will come from your willingness to take control of your life. How badly do you want it? Are you willing to adjust your focus to create the changes and reach the potential that you already own? After all, we are simply talking about *you* developing the best *you* possible. The discipline comes when you consistently stay in touch with your vision. To help you do this, you may develop habits and reminders. Saying grace or daily prayers may keep you in touch with your spirituality; leaving reminder notes on your mirror can help keep you focused on your goals. Regardless of what the habit is, simple reminders can be powerful.

Essentially, a clear, well-defined philosophy gives you the guidelines and boundaries that keep you on track. I recall Lou Tice giving me an example years ago—the difference between a bullet and a guided missile is that once a bullet is fired, it's out of anyone's control, but a guided missile is specifically designed to make course corrections. This is what a philosophy does for you—it helps you make the course corrections that you need.

Years ago in New England, as I searched for my personal truths, I remembered being a teenager reading a story in a magazine about future NBA Hall of Famer Rick Barry. As I recall the story, the writer was interviewing him during a shoot-around before a game. Rick was shooting jump shots as they talked, moving from left to right twenty-five times and from right to left twenty-five times, draining almost every shot from the top of the key. I have always remembered the question the reporter asked as well as the answer from Rick.

"Hey, Rick," the reporter asked. "Do you have a philosophy of life, or some principle that guides you?" Rick turned to him, with an arrogant look that was practically a trademark, and simply said, "Yeah—I'm a 46 percent lifetime shooter. If I miss my first ten shots, look out!"

I couldn't get that statement out of my head. It wasn't until years later that I came to realize the power you have when you truly know yourself. Even at the age of fifteen, I was struck by that statement and by what an extraordinary illustration of self-confidence it was. Rick was then only five years, give or take, into his fourteen-year NBA/ABA career. Just think about how well he must have known himself back then to espouse such an all-encompassing philosophy. He was saying, *I know myself so well that if I miss my first ten shots, you had better look out, because I know I'm going to make my next ten . . . give or take a few.* That wasn't a prediction; it was a statement of fact. That was who he was as an athlete. What an outlook on basketball, life, and the power of "knowing thyself." Imagine the power and authenticity he felt in that knowing. Certainty like that comes not merely from a high estimation of one's own talent, but from a deep knowledge of one's strengths and weaknesses. This principle has become one of the pillars of my philosophy both personally and professionally.

But the story doesn't end there.

I had just arrived at the San Francisco 49ers in 1995. Members of our staff were invited to the Bay Area Sports Hall of Fame banquet, an annual affair. I accompanied the group to enjoy a night out with many of the local sports legends and dignitaries and, at the break in the evening's festivities, whom did I happen to see but Rick Barry. My old hero was walking across the floor, being followed by a pack of autograph seekers, much to his dismay. I was struck with the thought: *Here's my chance. After all these years, I can finally ask Rick if he really had this philosophy of "If I miss my first ten shots, look out!"*

I hesitated for a minute and I told myself, *Aw, what the heck, you may never get this chance again. Go for it!* So I jumped out of my chair and joined the group of autograph seekers—no special access, just another fan. Feeling like a true groupie, I worked my way to Rick's side. He was looking quite perturbed by the whole scene, and I introduced myself as the new defensive coordinator of the 49ers, in hopes that might serve as a good icebreaker. Instead, he glanced at me with a skeptical glare that might as well have said, "Yeah, sure, buddy, and I'm Red Auerbach!"

Not to be denied this opportunity, I doggedly pressed on. Making myself heard over the crowd, I called out, "Hey, Rick, did you ever say that you're a 44 percent lifetime shooter, and if you miss your first ten shots, look out?" Now I had his attention. He looked at me as if he had just smelled something awful and replied, "I never said that!"

And in a flash, my life philosophy and all that I had validated it with was dashed! For a moment I felt foolish. After all, this mantra, which displayed Rick's confidence about himself, had been a huge thing for me, as I had adopted the mentality and come to rely upon it over the years. But then I thought, *No way am I going to let this break my spirit. This mantra has served me well, and I'll be damned if I'm not going to stick with it anyway! I don't need Rick Barry to validate my credo; I can think for myself.*

And in the next instant, as I was walking away, I heard Rick call out in my direction. I turned around. *Aha!* I thought, elated and relieved. *He's going to say he remembered making that statement after all, and he really did believe in it.*

Rick Barry looked into my expectant face, stared me dead in the eye, and said, "And besides, I was a *46* percent lifetime shooter!"

The overwhelming certainty Rick displayed on that occasion just blew me away. I felt as if I had been let in on one of the secrets to his success. Even today, I consider him to be one of the best examples of the direct link between someone knowing himself and being successful. When you truly know yourself, you have the best chance of using your strengths to your best advantage. And when things aren't going so well, it is so much easier to get back on track when you have a plan for where you want to go.

When I speak to young men and women coming out of high school or college who are just beginning to learn about themselves, I give them all the same advice: No matter what the task, what the job, compete to make yourself valuable at whatever you're doing. This work ethic is what makes it highly probable that good things will happen to you. Your first job experiences may not be what you've dreamed about, but there is intrinsic value in a job well done, and you will be recognized for that. Your real value comes from being dependable and resourceful, and someone is bound to notice. Know that you are always preparing for your very next job.

We are all different individuals. We all have different strengths and weaknesses, and not all of us have the same opportunities in life. The better we understand ourselves, the more informed we become about where it makes sense for us to focus our energies. That's why I encourage people to spend some time writing down words or phrases that describe their personality traits, values, dreams, goals, and more. I frequently challenge people to write down their personal philosophy as well, or at least give it a try.

It sounds like pretty basic stuff, but in reality it is anything but an easy process. If that process interests you then dig in and get ready to compete to find your truth—and don't be discouraged if it takes longer than you expected. Listen to your heart, trust your intuition, and allow yourself to be fascinated by the adventure of finding the real you. It's the journey to discover your personal truth that will make all the difference.

My own journey has led me to so many unexpected places and into so many unexpected roles—even that of poet. My theme? I'll give you one guess.

A few years ago, when the NCAA still allowed head coaches to recruit in the spring, I went to watch a talented high school running back named Dillon Baxter. It was baseball season, and as a freshman he was starting in center field on the varsity baseball team. Athletically, he was obviously a cut above the other players. His team was down a run going into the final inning and he was up with a runner on third. I was thinking, *There's no way this young kid is going to come through and win this game right here.* I had already evaluated him as an extraordinary football player in the fall, but could he be so special and hit a game-winning home run right in front of me? With two outs and the game on the line, he took two bad cuts and was quickly down in the count, 0–2. On the third pitch, he cracked a fastball to left center. My first thought was, *No way, it can't be . . .* The ball kept carrying, bringing the fans to their feet. As we were about to cheer for a home run, the opposing team's center fielder made an incredible catch, just before the wall. Dillon almost pulled it off, and needless to say, I walked away entirely impressed.

After the game, I was sitting on a plane heading to visit another recruit. I couldn't stop thinking about the baseball game and the young phenom I had just seen. He was only fourteen years old! I couldn't help but think about his next three years of high school and the pressure that would be on him in so many different ways. I began to text him, but soon realized that the message was too long, and way too emotional. So I saved it and wrote it down later. In a matter of minutes it was done, and I titled it "Always Compete."

Deciding not to send it, I just put it in my desk drawer. A year later, I pulled it out of that drawer to revisit my thoughts inspired by that young kid in San Diego. I realized that this was not a message just written for some superstar prospect but rather a message to send to every great young athlete we would ever recruit and every player on our team. I was writing this to remind them to be humble and keep their heads on straight while competing for their goals and dreams.

Furthermore, they should never hold back as they discover who they are and what they stand for.

During our 2007 team banquet, I finally decided to break it out, so I read this poem aloud. That senior class of twenty-three members had won five straight Pac-10 titles and had accomplished things that could only be done by great competitors. As they were moving on, I felt myself competing one final time to coach up our message to these players. As our saying goes, if you want to Win Forever, Always Compete.

ALWAYS COMPETE

Always Compete . . .

As you progress through your sporting life . . .

Always Compete.

If you want to go for it . . .

Always Compete.

You're gonna have to make choices in life and those choices need to be conscious decisions. There's only one person in control here, and that person is you . . .

You hold all the cards. You are the master of you. It's time to admit it . . .

You have always known this. So if you're ready, act on it . . .

Always Compete.

Don't you dare try to be too cool, don't you dare be afraid of life,

Just "dare to be great," and let it rip.

Always be humble, always be kind, always be respectful . . .

Always Compete.

Everything you do counts and screams who you are. There is no hiding from you.

Act as if the whole world will know who you are . . .

Always Compete.

Be true to yourself and let nothing hold you back.

Compete to be the greatest you, and that will always be enough and that will be a lifetime!

Always Compete.

CONCLUSION

The process of self-discovery, creating a vision, and competing to hold on to those ideals allowed my nine years at USC to be the most extraordinary years of my life. Yes, we won countless games and many championships, but to be honest, there are only a few football memories that really stick out.

I can vividly recall our first team meeting at the fifty-yard line. I remember when we turned around our first season at Arizona with a big win, the Orange Bowl victory over Oklahoma, and the epic fourth-and-nine play at South Bend. Of course, there are a few I would rather forget, such as the Texas game or the losses in my final season at USC, but my time in Heritage Hall was really never about individual moments. They won't be what I'll cherish as my life moves on, and they won't be the topic of conversation when I meet new friends in Seattle.

Rather, what will remain in my heart will be the journey that the USC football program allowed me to be a part of, from that first interview at the Sheraton Hotel near the airport to my final press conference when I resigned in January 2010. You see, life is never about singular moments because they are never enough to sustain pure happiness. Sure, postgame victory celebrations, Friday-night team meetings, and staff retreats are a blast, and I hope to have many more overlooking Seattle in the years to come, but life is about the journey.

Within that journey were incredible relationships that were made, friendships that were formed, and personal growth that was evident. Within that journey was watching players arrive as skinny, wide-eyed freshmen and leave as college graduates, NFL draft picks, or even free-agent signees. Within that journey were invitations to former players' weddings, pictures of their firstborn children, and random text messages saying thank you. Within that journey was watching young coaches accept coordinator and head coaching jobs at other institutions and teams. Within that journey was watching former members of the Bloods, Crips, and Mexican Mafia graduate from A Better LA's community-supported intervention training program. Within that journey was growth, discovery, and sheer joy.

So when I'm asked what I'll miss most about my time at USC and the Los Angeles Memorial Coliseum, it won't be the wins, and it surely won't be the losses. Instead, it will be the people—those who affected me and those whom I've been fortunate enough to affect.

You see, the beauty of life is that it doesn't stop. It keeps moving and keeps evolving, and as I look toward my next competitive challenge with the Seattle Seahawks, I can't help but feel reenergized, more enthusiastic, and as focused as I have ever been in my career.

Yet it is vital for me to share the reason why I am so excited. Not that I wasn't happy at USC, but why I left has everything to do with who I am at my core. I'm a competitor, and when I was weighing my options in January to either remain at USC or accept the position in Seattle, it became so clear to me what to do. I had to trust my intuition, my philosophy, and my vision, and that led me to what ended up being an obvious decision.

To be the vice president of football operations and head coach of the Seattle Seahawks is a dream job. To have the ability to make decisions, be innovative, and work with what will be known as the best front office in football is a perfect fit for my personality. It was obvious from the first interview with Tod Leiweke; in our hiring of our general manager, John Schneider; and in every off-season acquisition we've made, that this organization is committed "to do things better than they have ever been done before"—and everyone, and I mean everyone, will be on the same page.

Within the first month of my hiring, I took our entire organization of over three hundred employees through the Win Forever philosophy. To everyone from the coaching staff to college scouts to the marketing and sales teams, ticket managers, public relations staff, and the entire front office, I presented the methodology that our organization would now live by. It was an incredible moment as I stood in front of 150 staff members in our team meeting room and was streamed live to the other employees at Qwest Field. I could feel that they had been thirsting for a moment like this. Since then, I have been able to watch our approach resonate throughout the entire organization. The point was not to boast about the philosophy I had developed ten years ago. Rather, it was to be sure that when we take our first step as an organization, we take it together, as competitors.

I know that I will be evaluated in Seattle by wins and losses. That is the nature of the profession I've chosen for the last thirty-six years. But our record is not what motivates me to wake up and drive to the Seahawks training facility everyday.

What motivates me is the competition that this job offers and the competitive level that it requires on a daily basis. Years ago I was asked, "Pete, which is better: winning or competing?"

My response was instantaneous: "Competing . . . because it lasts longer."

As you watch our organization in Seattle take on new challenges this fall, I want you to watch for specifics. Follow our team during training camp and into our first game and, I hope, into the play-offs. You will know how we operate, how we speak, how we train, and how we compete. It won't be magic and it won't change the world, but it will be unique. We will be uniquely us. You should have a clear understanding of what we did while at USC and why we chose to use certain methods, and you can see the record of the success that came from that approach. Now, at the highest level of competition, you'll be able to see if we can take a team that won nine games in the past two years and change that culture. You'll be able to watch it unfold, with inside knowledge about what our philosophy entails and the competitive theme we will be following.

The Win Forever philosophy is successful because we set out a vision "to do things better than they have ever been done before," with competition being the central theme driving us to maximize our potential. But understand that competition does not need to be your theme. You have to find the philosophy and the vision and the theme that work for you. They are for you to discover, for you to embrace, and for you to accept. Make them yours. Live them to your fullest. Maximize *your* potential.

Win Forever.

I would love to hear your philosophy in twenty-five words or less, as well as the vision you created.

Please e-mail me at **PeteCarroll@WinForever.com**.

Acknowledgments

Acknowledging all the people who made this book possible takes me back to the early years of playing sports at home in Greenbrae. My brother Jim and our friends were always available and helped shape my love for playing sports. Regarding team sports, it began with my first football coach, John Pagliaro, as he instilled a pride and toughness that gave me the foundation and expectation for what competition was all about. Following him, I have to thank all of my early coaches who made the game fun and helped me want to play forever. My high school football coach, Bob Troppmann, took over from there, instilling pride and respect for the game. Along with my coaches, I was truly inspired by my early sports heroes such as Willie Mays, Gale Sayers, Rick Barry, and others and I have competed to be like them ever since childhood.

I must also thank my loving wife and best friend, Glena, as she enabled me to chase this dream of a lifetime with undying support and love. I could not have accomplished anything without her. She has held our loving family together and helped them become strong and independent, allowing us all to be best friends today.

The inspiration for this book came one day when I sat down in my office at USC with then assistant quarterback coach, Yogi Roth, and proceeded to map out a plan to generate revenue to help support my growing foundation, A Better LA. Yogi's first response was, "Well, you gotta write a book!" I said, "Okay, what else?" and we proceeded to fill a white board with ideas such as staging a peace rally, spreading A Better LA's message on *60 Minutes,* creating a sports academy for players and coaches, and developing an IMAX film about college football. These ideas have all come together with the book being an integral piece. Yogi was there at "inspiration" and has been there every step of the way in creating our Win Forever business. By sharing his extraordinary work ethic, creative talents, and competitiveness he has been the driving force in bringing our Win Forever philosophy to the world. Yogi eventually took charge of the enormous process of writing this book, and without him, it never would have made it into print.

Invaluable support came from my lifelong friend Dave Perron, as he helped me stay on course and maintain a balanced mentality when challenges arose. Dave also helped me assemble a fantastic group of advisers. Long-time friend Mark Jackson always kept me connected to the core of our philosophy as we created our plan together. Mark was with me at the outset and has been a steady force dating back to our beginnings in New England. Gary Uberstine has provided overall guidance, legal and business expertise, as well as unending loyalty, and has represented me for nearly twenty years.

Keith Sarkisian has brought us into the world of entertainment through his work at William Morris Endeavor Entertainment and has brought us countless opportunities and extraordinary insight. Andy Bark, who is widely known for shaping the industry of teen athlete development, has inspired us all as he implemented our philosophy within his business, now at ESPN RISE. Andy continues to consult for the corporate side of our Win Forever efforts and he has tremendous value. Entrepreneur Michael Gale has given us a global scope and outlook that will continue to shape our vision for the future.

Our Win Forever collaboration has been a joyous one with our team believing in the vision we set in motion and bringing it to life. I am so grateful for their loyalty and support in all ways.

To the numerous coaches I have been honored to work with and support—the friendships and the fun have always been worth the struggles. Through the wins and losses I have learned that my favorite part of coaching has been the relationships.

Without the support of Portfolio publishing, Adrian Zackheim's vision, and Courtney Young's dedication this book would not have been possible. To them and their staff, thank you. Also, Kristoffer Garin's aid in the early stages of this manuscript were instrumental and facilitated the project. Also, I'd like to thank Jay Mandel of William Morris Endeavor Entertainment for managing this project from start to finish.

Finally, without the hundreds of players, their dedication and desire to perform every day on the field, in the weight room, and in the classroom, there would be no competition and no reason to formulate a philosophy, so I must say thank you.

It is not possible to acknowledge everyone properly, but to all of those who took part in this, thanks for making it all come to life.

Index